CONFUCIUS FOR CHRISTIANS

CONFUCIUS FOR CHRISTIANS

WHAT AN ANCIENT CHINESE WORLDVIEW CAN TEACH US ABOUT LIFE IN CHRIST

GREGG A. TEN ELSHOF

WILLIAM B. EERDMANS PUBLISHING COMPANY
Grand Rapids, Michigan / Cambridge, U.K.

Published 2015 by
WM. B. EERDMANS PUBLISHING CO.
2140 Oak Industrial Drive N.E., Grand Rapids, Michigan 49505 /
P.O. Box 163, Cambridge CB3 9PU U.K.

Library of Congress Cataloging-in-Publication Data

Ten Elshof, Gregg A., 1970-
Confucius for Christians: what an ancient Chinese worldview
can teach us about life in Christ / Gregg A. Ten Elshof.
pages   cm
ISBN 978-0-8028-7248-7 (pbk.: alk. paper)
1. Christianity and other religions — Confucianism.
2. Confucianism — Relations — Christianity.
I. Title.
BR128.C43T45   2015
261.2'9512 — dc23

2015017964

www.eerdmans.com

CONTENTS

ACKNOWLEDGMENTS

THIS BOOK, MORE than anything else I've ever written, is not my own. It is the product of countless conversations over the past ten years or so. I am so very grateful to Dr. Thomas Leung for introducing me to the beauty and power of the Confucian wisdom tradition and for inspiring reflection on its relationship to the Way of Jesus. I'm also grateful to Gary Miller for dragging me into the unknown. Many of the ideas in the book were shaped in a seminar that I taught in the Spring of 2013 at Biola University. This book belongs in part to the students of that seminar. I'm especially grateful to Louys Gackstetter for his help in pulling things together. Though my conversation partners concerning this book are too numerous to remember or mention, I do wish to thank the following friends and colleagues for their patience with me and for their help as I worked through these ideas: Andrew Bailey, David Bratt, Jason Baehr, Thomas Crisp, Melodie Holden, Jim Houston, Jasmeet Kennington, Michael Pace, Steven Porter, Dan Speak, Dallas Willard, and Amos Yong.

I'm grateful to have received from Biola University a sabbatical leave to complete the manuscript. And I'm forever grateful to God for Laurel, Silas, Larkin, and Gideon. This center of love infuses everything I do with joy and meaning.

Acknowledgments

Finally, the book is dedicated to my parents, Gene and Judy Ten Elshof who, by generously and effortlessly giving themselves to me and to countless others, beautifully embody many of the principles discussed in these pages.

CHAPTER 1

CONFUCIAN CHRISTIANITY?

I WAS BORN A Christian. And I was born a Westerner.

Of course, there's a perfectly good sense in which neither of those things could be true. We all know that you can't be born a Christian any more than you can be born a Marxist. And the same goes for the tendency to think in categories given to us from the Western wisdom tradition.

On the other hand, I've understood the world in Christian categories for as long as it has made sense to say of me that I've understood the world. I've been thinking in Christian categories for as long as I've been thinking. While I've had a conversion experience, I've never had a conversion experience that took me from some wholly other way of thinking about and understanding the world to a Christian way. Nor have I ever had a conversion experience that took me for the first time into a basic orientation of loyalty to and trust in the person of Jesus Christ. I've embodied a basic orientation of loyalty and trust toward Jesus Christ for as long as it has made sense to say of me that I've trusted anything or manifested loyalty to anyone. Such are the blessings of being raised in a Christian home. And the same is true of the Western wisdom tradition. Long before I had ever heard of Socrates, Plato, and Aristotle (not to mention Aquinas, Descartes, Hume,

Kant, and Kierkegaard), my thinking had been deeply shaped by their suggestions about how to understand and talk about the world and my place in it.

So I've been thinking as a Western Christian for as long as I've been thinking.

It took me what now seems like an alarmingly long time to situate myself in those terms — to see and appreciate the fact that the Western wisdom tradition is one among many, and that a Christian understanding of the world informed by Western philosophical categories and emphases is one among many ways of understanding the world as a Christian. To deviate from stereotypical Western patterns of thinking is not to be unthinking. And to deviate from stereotypical Western Christian thinking is not to abandon Christianity.

Perhaps all of this should go without saying. But when I reflect on my own intellectual journey, it occurs to me that, at least in many settings, it must be said. I'm not sure where or when, but at some point in my intellectual training I took aboard the suggestion that the word "Eastern," when used to modify nouns like "philosophy," "thought," or "religion," had connotations like these: illogical, uncritical, nonsensical, relativistic, and dangerous. But a moment's reflection is all it takes to recognize the absurdity of the suggestion that a philosopher's location on the globe (To the East — of what? one wonders) should conduce to any of these characteristics. Be that as it may, this is how I had been taught to think.

It is, of course, not absurd to suggest that some religions, philosophies, and patterns of thought are illogical, uncritical, nonsensical, relativistic, and dangerous. Sadly, our world is replete with religions, philosophies, and patterns of thought that satisfy each (if not all) of these descriptors. But that these patterns should be concentrated on one half of the globe (the East side) is what should strike us as implausible on its face. And it takes no more than an undergraduate-level survey of the history of Western thought to confirm the prevalence of these characteristics on the West side.

In 2005, the Provost of my university asked me to accompany him to China. The plan was to travel to several universities in Mainland China to give presentations to student and faculty groups on the nature of Christian higher education and scholarship. I had no real desire to go to China. I knew nothing of China's history or culture. But my boss' boss' boss was asking me to go. So who was I to say no?

Our guide was Dr. Thomas Leung, a Christian scholar who had been working hard to establish centers for the study of Christianity in the state universities in China. He was the first person I had ever met who self-identified both as a Christian and as a Confucian. This intrigued me.

In one of my early conversations with Dr. Leung, he explained one of the challenges facing Western Christian missionary efforts in China over the years. Well-meaning Western missionaries, in their attempt to make a Christian understanding of the world compelling, were unknowingly busy trying to propagate Western Christianity — Christianity articulated in categories and with emphases at home in the Western philosophical tradition. As a result, Chinese audiences were being asked not only to embrace Christian thinking, but to abandon their native Confucian wisdom tradition — a rich tradition stretching back thousands of years and which informs the most fundamental structures of life and social interaction in China.

Audiences in the West are not characteristically presented with such stark options. Because the Christian story is articulated in categories and with emphases at home in the Western philosophical tradition, these audiences are offered the opportunity to embrace the Christian story without wholesale abandonment of the rich wisdom tradition that stretches back to Socrates and Plato and informs the most fundamental structures of life and social interaction in the West.

If, as it has been often suggested, the whole of the Western philosophical tradition is a series of footnotes to Plato, then most Christians in the West — insofar as their thinking is informed by the Western philosophical tradition — are Platonic Christians whether they've heard of Plato or not. But if the Chinese philosophical tradition is a series of footnotes to Confucius, then why should there not be Confucian Christians as well?

This is not to say that everything that Plato or Confucius taught can be reconciled with the claims of Christianity. But is there any reason on the face of it to think that the wisdom tradition that developed in the East should be more difficult to reconcile with Christianity than is the wisdom tradition that developed in the West?

In any case, Dr. Leung's diagnosis of Western missionary efforts in China sparked in me a curiosity about the Confucian wisdom tradition and about the possibility of integrating Confucian categories and emphases with Christian commitment. In the years since that first trip to China, I've been studying the Confucian tradition. I've found it compelling and beautiful in many ways. And I think I've been brought further up and further into the Way of Jesus as a consequence of having interacted with it. I understand better now than I did several years ago what it might mean to be a "Confucian Christian." This book is a collection of my reflections along the way. My hope is that they will, in some small way, allow those already moving in the Confucian way to see how a life of Jesus-following might be understood in familiar terms. Closer to home, my hope is that folks who have come up in environments like mine (Western Christian folks who've been trained into suspicion of anything from the East) will find that there is much that is deep and helpful in the Confucian tradition — that reflections on the teachings of Confucius can inspire a deeper and richer understanding of our master and savior, Jesus Christ.

A word is in order here about how this book compares with other books and book chapters written by Christian authors on Confucianism. These usually fall into two categories:

First there are the Christian apologists. The apologists treat Confucianism as one of the world's great religions. As such, Confucianism competes with Christianity (and all of the other religions) for the allegiance of would-be practitioners. The apologists typically emphasize what they take to be the important differences between Christian thought and Confucian thought and recommend siding with Christianity.

Second, there are the Christian pluralists. The pluralists think that all of the world's great religions represent equally legitimate expressions of the human response to the Divine (or to Being or to The Real or whatever). The Christian pluralist, while self-identifying with the Christian tradition, will not think of this identification as having any privilege, advantage, or priority *vis-a-vis* an identification with one (or more) of the other great religions. These writers typically emphasize what they take to be the similarities between the world's great religions.

There are plenty of books authored by Christians that address Confucianism from the perspective of the apologist or the pluralist.

This book, though, is intended neither as a contribution to Christian apologetics nor to Christian pluralism. These approaches have in common that they treat Confucianism as one of the world's great religions — either one that competes with Christianity or one that is on equal footing with Christianity.

But it's a matter of some controversy among scholars whether or not Confucianism is, in fact, a religion. The question turns on complicated issues having to do with the defining marks of a religion. I'll not interact with those issues in this book. What is *not* controversial is that Confucianism (whether or not it is a religion) is a deep and influential wisdom tradition. And there are embarrassingly few books written from a Christian perspective that explore the possibility of integrating this deep and powerful tradition with a life of Jesus-following.

So in this book, we'll interact with Confucianism as a wisdom tradition — more like Platonism than like Islam. Confucianism will be thought of as one trajectory of thought to which to turn for deep reflection on the great questions that move human culture — questions about our world and our place in it. This book seeks neither to highlight the differences between Confucianism and Christianity nor to argue that there are no points of tension between the two. It rather seeks to experiment with reflection on perennial questions of human interest with the teachings of Jesus and Confucius in mind.

As a Christian, my fundamental allegiance is to Jesus Christ. For most of my adult life, I've helped myself to categories and emphases characteristic of the Western wisdom tradition in my attempt to think carefully about what a life of Jesus-following looks like. While I've not found the thought patterns of the Western philosophical tradition univocally friendly to Christian commitment and practice, I have found much to appreciate in the Western tradition and I'm better, and better equipped for following Jesus, for having studied it and taken aboard much of what I learned. In recent years, I've been helped in new ways by reflection on the Confucian tradition in the East. The following pages represent my attempt to articulate some of the dimensions along which I've been helped.

In a conversation with some students not long ago, my friend Tom put forward the suggestion that we approach the world's great wisdom traditions as scientists of the good life. Just as a Christian biologist might study and reflect on the body of collected human knowledge concerning biological organisms in order better to fulfill the biblical mandate to care for the created order, we mine the great traditions of sincere human reflection on the human condition for anything that can be of assistance in our attempt to understand deeply who we are, how our world works, and how best to fulfill the biblical mandate to promote human flourishing.

This is not a commentary (Christian or otherwise) on the Confucian *Analects*. It's not nearly so systematic or complete as all of that. It's rather an attempt to give expression to those ideas in the Confucian tradition that have been helpful for me as I've tried to make my way further up and into the Way of Jesus. My hope is that you will be similarly helped as you read them.

CHAPTER 2

FAMILY

*The gentleman applies himself to the roots. Once the roots are
firmly established, the Way will grow. Might we not say that
filial piety and respect for elders constitute the root of Goodness?*

ANALECTS 1.2

*While Jesus was still talking to the crowd, his mother and broth-
ers stood outside, wanting to speak to him. Someone told him,
"Your mother and brothers are standing outside, wanting to
speak to you." He replied to him, "Who is my mother, and who
are my brothers?" Pointing to his disciples, he said, "Here are my
mother and my brothers. For whoever does the will of my Father
in heaven is my brother and sister and mother."*

MATTHEW 12:46-50

J AY SITS ALONE in his spacious den, watching from his window
as the workers prepare the yard of his West Egg mansion for tonight's gala. The colors are bright. The mood is carefree and festive.
No expense is spared. Tonight's party, like all of Jay's parties, will be
the talk of the town. Jay himself, though, will not be poolside enjoying the festivities. He'll not suffer the risk of exposure that comes

with drinking even a little too much. He'll spend the evening where he is right now. Window-side, watching the party unfold. Aloof. Alone. Unknown. The guests too will be profoundly alone, even as they rub shoulders with one another poolside. F. Scott Fitzgerald offers this memorable description of the scene through the eyes of Jay's would-be protégé, Nick: "The bar is in full swing, and floating rounds of cocktails permeate the garden outside, until the air is alive with chatter and laughter, and a casual innuendo and introductions forgotten on the spot, and enthusiastic meetings between women who never knew each other's names."

Likewise, Babette is making elaborate preparations for a grand party. Once again, no expense is too great. The event will be the very picture of exorbitance and excess. The wine will flow and the feast will be endless. The mood will be carefree and festive. The upcoming extravagance is the talk of the town. Neighbors gossip, offering to one another their best guess at the outrageous cost of the imported quail and the bottles of Clos de Vougeot. Babette's feast, though, will have exactly the opposite effect on the citizens of Jutland as will Jay's party on the citizens of West Egg. Babette's guests will leave more deeply known than when they came. With each ladle of Potage a Tortue their hearts will be knit more tightly together. Babette, too, will be known in new ways at the feast. She will have, as Karen Blixen so beautifully puts it, that rare chance to do her utmost that is throughout the world the "one long cry from the heart of the artist." Hers is an outpouring of the soul, an invitation to true community. Jay's is an escape from the intimacy of the small party into the privacy of the crowd. We are drawn to Babette's feast as an expression of who we are and who we are created to be. Jay Gatsby's party, on the other hand, is an aberration, a twisting of delight that takes himself and others one step further from being fully human.

Trinitarian Christians have every reason to expect that Babette's feast would resonate deeply with what we all know to be beautiful and valuable in life — that it would strike us as deeply human. At the center of everything, according to the Trinitarian Christian story, is a community of persons enjoying one another in a perfect bond of self-giving love. This community of persons gave birth to Adam — a being somehow partaking in the capacity for the kind of community enjoyed by the trinity. Adam and his descendants were created for deep and meaningful relationship with similarly created beings and with the communal being to which they all owe their existence. The vision for this beautiful creative overflow of divine community would find expression in Jesus's summary of the law. Love God. Love each other. All else is to be in the service of love. Every extravagant expression of the artist, if it is not in the service of love, is the garish distraction of a party at the Gatsby mansion, a clanging cymbal.

It's a point not infrequently made that the Western philosophical tradition, at least in its dominant streams since the Enlightenment, has led us away from a deep appreciation for the degree to which being human *is* being in relationship. To be alone is to be less than fully human. Descartes' *ego,* the "I" of whose existence he could be so absolutely certain, is not human — not a descendent of Adam. This monad, this-thing-considered-alone, is no expression of the overflow of divine community that was and continues to be declared good by its maker. It is an abstraction, the focus upon which has given us the aberration that is the Western Individual — self-sufficient but not fully human. We are drawn to Babette's feast (and repulsed by the Great Gatsby) in part because our hearts long for the kind of community for which they were created. All of this is known well by the many who've reflected on the excesses of Western individualism.

But what can be done? Steeped as we are in the patterns of

thought and life shaped by an individualistic heritage, how can we find our way into something more human?

Sandy is thirty-eight. Her parents split up when she was six and shared custody of her until she graduated high school. Each spent much of their time with Sandy trying to convince her that the influence of the other was something she'd need to overcome. So Sandy could never fully embrace either those dimensions of her personality inherited from her mother or those that came to her from her father. There was one point of shared vision between her parents, though, for Sandy's life. She would need to work hard to excel in school. She should endeavor to find a good career in order not to be dependent on a man for her livelihood. Marriage, as she was well aware, is no safe bet for flourishing. So she excelled in school, went to college, earned graduate degrees in business and law and, a few years ago, made partner at her firm. Sandy had arrived. And she was deeply unhappy.

She's a good person. There are no glaring moral failings to be blamed for her deep unhappiness. But she is far from flourishing.

An acquaintance at the relatively large church she attends suggested to her that she needed relationships. Life, this friend suggested, is not meant to be lived alone. She was encouraged to "plug in" to the church community by joining an adult Sunday-school group comprising mostly other thirty-somethings.

Sandy's been meeting with these folks on Sunday mornings now for about four years. It's a pleasant experience. The meeting lasts ninety minutes. There's about twenty-five minutes of mingling over coffee and pastries followed by some announcements and prayer requests. Then a speaker. Then a few more minutes of mingling until the next service starts and another group is scheduled to occupy the room. It's nice to have a wider group of acquaintances. And there is the occasional party at someone's house where there is no speaker so the mingling can go uninterrupted for a couple of hours.

Still, Sandy is profoundly lonely. And she's not the only one. It's been challenging (to put it mildly) for churches in the West to counteract the deeply entrenched individualism, and the corresponding loneliness, of our intellectual heritage. We've been about the business for some time of helping individuals to be good. And the dominant strategy for addressing the hole that Sandy and countless others feel is to add friendships — small groups — to the mix. We add to our attempt to make *individuals* good the opportunity for *individuals* to be friends. But, for many, these attempts are falling short of addressing the deep and persistent loneliness they feel.

For the Confucian, on the other hand, the idea of a "good person" — a good *individual* — who lacks only the joy of significant human relationship is a foreign one. To fail to be in relationship — and to do relationship well — is to fail at being human. To grow in goodness you must find your way increasingly into the full expression of what you are. And a human person *just is* a being-in-relationship. A life devoid of significant and well-ordered relationships can no more be human than can an organism devoid of a root system be a tree. We can bring before our minds, of course, only that part of the tree that exists above the ground. But when we do, we are not considering the tree. We are considering a part of the tree. And the part of the tree we are considering could not exist and have the sort of being it has (the being of a tree) without its roots. Similarly, we can bring before our minds only that part of the human person that we call the "individual" — the thing you get when you abstract away from relationships with other persons. But when we do, we are not considering a human person. And the thing we *are* considering could not exist and have the sort of being it has (the being of a human person) apart from its relationship to other persons.

So, for the Confucian, growing into human goodness and growing into well-ordered relationships with others are not two separable projects as they are so often treated in the West. Making progress into the full expression of a human life well-lived *just is* making progress into a human life increasingly characterized by propriety in the various relationships that comprise the human condition. If we wish to be good, we must grow in our ability to be together. This is why filial piety is at the center of virtue — the root of goodness — for the Confucian. It's also why reflection on the Confucian Way may inspire deeper remedies for the profound loneliness so characteristic of contemporary Western life.

According to Confucius, there are five basic relationships, the mastery of which will facilitate flourishing for the human person. If we learn to live well into these five relational dynamics, thought Confucius, we'll be well positioned to flourish in any of the complex array of relational circumstances that come to us in life. The five relationships are these:

1. Ruler and subject.
2. Father and son.
3. Elder brother and younger brother.
4. Husband and wife.
5. Friend and friend.

Three of the five basic relationships are generated by inclusion in a family. For that reason, the family is the primary venue for growth into the full expression of being human for the Confucian. One learns how properly to negotiate the power dynamics associated with being a mother, a son, an older or younger sibling, a husband or a wife. And in so doing, one is increasingly well-positioned to grow into healthy relationships with friends, with subordinates, and with supervisors. The deep cure for loneliness — the path to genuine belonging — runs through the process of learning how to live well into the various dynamics that make for family life. Learn how to be a good daughter and you will know how to negotiate the dynamics of being a good employee. Learn to be a good father and you will know how to be a good supervisor. Learn to be a good younger sibling and you will know how to receive instruction from a teacher while maintaining a healthy degree of autonomy. It is in the context of the family that we acquire the building blocks for navigating the wildly complex relational networks that comprise human society.

A couple of years ago, I taught an undergraduate college course that covered the Confucian *Analects*. Most of the students were between the ages of nineteen and twenty-one. I presented the idea that sons and daughters in the Confucian Way, while they are afforded the opportunity to respectfully remonstrate, are expected finally, and absent obviously aberrant conditions, to submit to the wishes of their parents. I asked how many of them found this an attractive ideal. Almost everyone did. They were thinking of children.

Then I made it clear to them that, in the Confucian Way, sons and daughters had this kind of submission enjoined upon them until well after their parents had died. That is, I made it clear to them that the Confucian Way includes submission to parents well into adulthood. The resulting departure of sympathy in the room for the Confucian Way was palpable. I asked how many of them had it as a part of their vision for life into adulthood that they would, in significant ways, continue in submission to their parents. I made it clear that submission means doing what the person to whom you're submitted advises even when it goes against your own considered judgments. You do not "invite and take seriously the advice" of someone to whom you are submitted in order to ultimately do what you, yourself, think is best. You do what they say.

Alarmingly few of them had anything like submission as a part of their ideal for adulthood. Submission is just the thing for kids, they thought, but part of what it means to be an adult is to make one's own choices. Mature adults will, of course, invite and take seriously the council of wise others including parents (if, indeed, one is lucky enough to have wise parents — a remarkably rare occurrence, it would seem, from the testimony of these students). But, at the end of the day, an adult makes her own choices.

Then I asked at what age one could be expected to graduate from a life of submission to a life of autonomy of the sort they envisioned. The answer? Between the ages of nineteen and twenty-one.

Clearly, the ideas of autonomy and maturity were fused in the minds of these undergraduate students. At the ripe age of twenty, they thought, one is ready to weigh in the balance all of the considerations that make for responsible life-making and to strike out on one's own. One has after two whole decades, I suppose, absorbed enough of the wisdom that has been collected over the millennia of human existence to evaluate advice from peers and elders and discern the best course of action for oneself.

Of course, Christians should have nothing to do with the conflation of autonomy and maturity. If it's autonomy you seek, you should go in for some other religion. The Christian vision of heaven is one of eternal submission to the Father. And if this life is to be a sort of training for the life to come, we don't do ourselves any favors by encouraging our youth into a life of autonomy at the age of twenty-one. We would do better to train them to be good sons and daughters — to navigate with increasing facility the balance between free expression of their uniqueness and the submission appropriate to their existence as sons, as daughters, as employees, as created beings. To think otherwise is to train them to be gods. And gods they will never be.

So the family is God's gift to us. It is the natural training ground for increasingly free expression of one's uniqueness in the context of the various dimensions of appropriate submission. And it is an idiosyncratic fiction of the contemporary West to think that the natural and appropriate conclusion for this training coincides with becoming legally able to consume alcohol or to get married. There are conditions, of course, under which it is necessary for one's own mental health to find distance from one's family of origin (biological or otherwise). But to scorn one's family is to abandon something for which there is likely to be no easy replacement. And to scorn one's family for its imperfections in search of the perfect venue for relationship training is to chase after a pipe dream. The imperfections of human society ensure that every family — every social environment — will be an imperfect setting for our training. As imperfect as your family is, it may be the best and most natural place for you to grow into the kind of person who can relate well to the others with whom it has been given you to live.

But didn't Jesus teach that we'll often need to scorn our mothers and brothers if we're to follow him? Well, no. He didn't. But to understand what Jesus *did* teach about family, we need to understand that there are two opposite errors one must avoid when it comes to the priority of family and filial piety. First, an emphasis on filial piety can devolve into a kind of clannish exclusivity. Folks sometimes grow into a perspective that fails to take seriously into account their relationships to anyone *except* those in their family. Second, and often in an attempt to avoid the first kind of error, folks sometimes fail to do justice to — to give appropriate time, energy, and attention to — living well into the relational dynamics of their family.

What the errors have in common is the failure to recognize the family as the model for appropriate human relatedness more generally. Those who've fallen into the first error never get beyond family — never fully appreciate that the clan is there to train them into loving dispositions capable of extending *beyond* the clan. Those who've fallen into the second error move too quickly or thoroughly beyond the clan. They think they can achieve the good life — good relationships, growth in virtue, love for neighbor — without continual training toward mastery in the basic relationships that comprise family.

In the gospels, we find Jesus inaugurating his Messianic Kingdom with a group that had fallen squarely into the first of these two errors. First-century Jewish culture (indeed, first-century Mediterranean culture generally) was inordinately family-centric. The clannish exclusivity that had grown up in that culture had caused a kind of group blindness to the multi-national blessing that was to pour out of the Jewish nation. Just as families exist to train us for more expansive love, the Jewish nation was called together to be a source of expansive blessing to all the nations. But, having fallen into the first of our two errors, first-century Jewish culture was stuck at the level of family, of tribe. And Jesus, as is often the case with his teaching, says what needs saying in order to jolt them out of their particular error.

So, when given the opportunity, Jesus repeatedly makes it plain and public that his project extends beyond family — certainly beyond his family of origin and even beyond the ethnic family of Israel. Because Israel had fallen into the first kind of error, following Jesus into a more expansive program of love would certainly have felt like scorn for family to anyone caught up in that culture. Paul (in a slightly less aggressive way) picks up the same theme when he encourages the multi-ethnic churches he'd planted to address one another in fa-milial terms — to greet one another as "brother." To do this, as a first-century Jew, would have been an outrage. It would have been considered shameful and disrespectful to one's true brothers. Paul, though, was trying to lift the Jewish church out of the clannish dis-position they'd inherited from their ethnic identity. He was helping them to extend the love so thoroughly developed in the family to those beyond it.

For all of his attempt to free his Jewish audience from their insular clannish way, though, Jesus never departed from his basic orientation of filial piety. His position was complicated (to put it mildly) by the fact that the submissive orientation appropriate to being a son was transferred to his heavenly Father. He remained submissive to his Father to the end. He went after the Pharisees and teachers of the law for allowing their supposed devotion to God to stand in the way of caring appropriately for aging parents. And he never forsook the loving filial posture of an adult son to his aging mother. Among his last words and thoughts (precious words and thoughts, no doubt, for someone putting into effect the final stages of the atonement that would rescue the entire world from sin) were those directed toward the care of his mother upon his death. Jesus was a faithful and filial son both to his earthly mother and to his heavenly Father.

But the first error — the error into which Jesus' audience had fallen — is *not* the error of the contemporary West. The idea, utterly foreign to the first-century Jewish mind, that one could be a basically good person who had (either through decision or through simple un-intentional drift) come to have nearly nothing to do with one's family is commonplace in the contemporary West. When someone in their forties announces in conversation that they have virtually nothing to do with their family anymore (or with this or that member of their family), we don't find ourselves naturally concluding that they, themselves, are living far from virtue — far from the good life. Indeed, if someone says that they're estranged from one or more members of their family, it's tempting to think in response, "who isn't?" Nobody thinks it a bad idea, of course, to honor one's family. And everyone knows that growing up in a dysfunctional family has the potential to detract from the good life well into adulthood. But, for all of that, a life of continued thriving relational wholeness with one's family of origin into adulthood is, to the contemporary Western mind, accidental at best to a life of flourishing.

It is the second of our two errors, then, that dominates the contemporary Western landscape. Far from falling into a kind of clannish exclusivity that prevents our caring for anyone beyond those in our families, we've neglected to appreciate the centrality of the family for loving those beyond it well. We're trying to establish significant and healthy relationships with friends, neighbors, superiors, and the world without having made much progress in the mastery of the basic relational dynamics given us insofar as we are fathers, mothers, sons, daughters, older and younger siblings, and spouses. We're tempted to think that we can somehow manage to love the world without having learned to love well those whom have been given to us as family. Reflection on the Confucian emphasis on filial piety can function as a kind of corrective here. The Confucian would remind us that if we wish to love the world, we'll need to attend carefully to the "root" of love — the root of goodness. We'll need to continually work at wholeness in the basic familial relationships.

First-century Jews needed to be reminded that relational wholeness in the family, while a good and beautiful thing in itself, is intended to conduce to relational wholeness with those beyond the family. In fact, for the Confucian, the better you love your family, the more capable and effective will be your love for those beyond your family. But in a culture caught up in the first of our two errors — the error of clannish exclusivity — the call to this expansion of love beyond your family will feel like a call to dishonor or neglect your family. Insofar as Jesus was calling his audience out of clannish exclusivity and into a more expansive love, he was calling them to a life that would have *felt,* given their training, like scorn and dishonor for family.

Contemporary Western culture is in the opposite position. We need to be reminded that love of the world and a life lived in meaningful relationships with others, while beautiful, have as their foundations the mastery of the basic relationships that comprise family. The heart well-trained in the love and power dynamics that animate family life is the heart most adequately equipped for love of neighbor, the world, and even the enemy. We need to be reminded, for example, that mastering the art of being a younger sibling can prepare one to affect a loving response to a disrespectful teacher or that learning to remonstrate from the submissive posture of the filial son can prepare us to grow under the direction of a priest with whom we have significant disagreements about theology or church life.

There are, then, these two errors. On one hand, Jesus' first-century Jewish audience had fallen into clannish exclusivity. Jesus' call to a more expansive love would have been mistaken for a call to scorn for one's family. On the other hand, Western individualistic culture has fallen into the error of neglecting the significance of family as the natural and primary place to grow into the relational skills that make for human flourishing. And the call of Confucius to a more intense focus on filial piety is easily mistaken for a call to slavish parochialism and the neglect of things and people beyond one's own family. Both of these mistakes — the mistake of thinking that Jesus endorses scorn for family and the mistake of thinking that Confucius endorses neglect of those outside one's family — owe in part to the mistake of thinking that love is a zero-sum game. The mistake is to think that I've got a fixed quantity of love to unleash on the world and that mine is the difficult choice of how to divide that love between my family members, my neighbors, my enemies, and the world beyond my immediate acquaintance.

My wife's second pregnancy was at least as scary for me as was her first, but for different reasons. My son Silas was almost two. And I was experiencing for the first time that approximation of divine selfless love that so many parents report. I understood in new ways what it was to stand ready without hesitation to give my life for another. I remember the amazement with which I discovered this capacity for felt selflessness in myself. Marriage had taken me some distance from my stubborn selfishness. But parenthood was a quantum leap. I remember the amazement with which I looked at this infant — this person that I barely knew — with a kind of certainty that I would give anything at all for his flourishing. My fear, typical from what I gather from other parents, was that my father-love was entirely spent on this boy for whom I would sacrifice the world. I felt I had nothing left to offer a second child. And the thought of somehow *splitting* the love, devotion, and energy currently directed upon Silas between him and a second child was abhorrent to me. What I hadn't yet learned, and what every parent with more than one child can verify, is that love is not a zero-sum game.

The truth is that my father-love *was* entirely spent on Silas. I had nothing left to give by way of the devotion, investment, and loyalty of a father. But as my daughter, Larkin, grew in her mother's womb and eventually joined us my heart grew with her. I didn't need to love Silas less, to be somehow less devoted to or invested in him, in order to love and devote myself to Larkin with the same degree of intensity. My heart had expanded to accommodate my full measure of father-love for each. By the time Laurel was pregnant with our third child, I had learned the lesson. I had none of the sort of fear I experienced during her pregnancy with Larkin. While my resources for father-love were entirely spent on Larkin and Silas, I had learned and I knew that my heart would grow even as Gideon grew in his mother's womb and eventually joined us. I had learned that love is not a zero-sum game.

The call of Jesus, far from a call to scorn one's family, is a call to realize that our hearts were created to grow in such a way as to be capable of increasingly expansive horizons of love. Though our love *may be* entirely spent on the clan it's an illusion to think that loving our neighbors, our enemies, and the world will entail a rationing off of the love currently devoted to family. Our hearts can grow to fully accommodate both. And the call of Confucius, far from a call to neglect of those outside our clan, is a call to realize that our best resources for growing into an expansive heart for the world come to us in the context of family. When we have virtually nothing to do with our families (either by decision or by virtue of mere drift in pursuit, say, of career or other life goals), we disassociate ourselves from the root of the good human life — the life of rich community and relational wholeness. Our ethical convictions may drive us to a life of beneficence and charitable contribution here and there. Our *influence* for others may be wide and praiseworthy so far as they go if we've got considerable resources and strong ethical convictions. But our capacity for *love* will be underdeveloped.

Contemporary Western culture — and by extension, contemporary Western Christianity — stands in desperate need of this Confucian call. The radical individualism of our intellectual heritage makes it very unlikely that we'll fall into anything like a clannish exclusivity with regard to our family of origin. Families in the contemporary West slip in and out of familial bonds with alarming fluidity. They abandon their investment in one another, it seems, at the drop of a hat. In families where I come from, for example, folks have abandoned filial piety over a disagreement about which protestant reformed church to attend (not, mind you, over whether or not to be protestant or even over whether or not to be protestant reformed, but over which kind of protestant reformed church). Others, who've made no conscious decision to abandon filial piety, have simply drifted away from the investment, loyalty, and devotion characteristic of the flourishing family. They still see one another, of course, at those set times when families are supposed to meet (Christmas, Easter, birthdays, and the like). But the meetings are just so many gatherings of individuals at a Gatsby party — often reinforcing the profoundly-felt aloneness characteristic of life outside the meetings.

And nobody really thinks twice about it. Nobody will question your basic integrity and goodness — your likely capacity for wide love — upon hearing that you've drifted away from your family of origin. In fact, it's hard to find anyone at all who can report having lived a whole life in the context of deep investment, loyalty, and devotion to father, mother, sons and daughters, grandparents, siblings, spouse, uncles, aunts and cousins. Our entire way of being, it seems, simply assumes that this will *not* be the case.

Jesus urged his students towards an extension of the profound bonds of family to one another but without regard for clan. Paul picked up this theme and encouraged his churches to apply familial categories to one another. The call was to deep communal investment, loyalty, and devotion to one another as fellow practitioners of the Way initiated in the life and teachings of Jesus. The invitation was to take what they were *already doing* in the context of family and apply it to the communities forming around discipleship to Jesus.

So what do you get when you invite folks steeped in the contemporary Western posture toward family to apply what they're *already doing* in the context of family to their Christian communities — when you invite them to *be* extended family for one another? Perhaps you get an association of folks who think of themselves in largely autonomous and individualistic terms and who slide in and out of connection with different churches over the years depending on where their life's pursuits, interests, and preferences take them. They'll appreciate being a part of a group, of course. Nobody wants to be alone. But it will be the rare bird who remains with any one group over a lifetime. They'll drift in and out of various associations, driven by their other priorities in life. Their investment in the group with which they're currently connected will likely be structured around set times when it is expected that there should be a meeting; Sunday mornings perhaps. And many will be as lonely at the meeting (perhaps even more lonely) as they are during the course of the week.

Jesus and Paul had something entirely different in mind. They were calling together communities united around the practice of the Way of Jesus. They had it in mind that these communities would give themselves to one another with the long-lasting loyalty, investment, and devotion then characteristic of the extended family. These would not be loose and relatively short-lived associations of autonomous individuals. These would be groups living life together; groups for whom the thought of me-without-this-community would have the same structure as a thought of only that part of the tree that exists above the ground.

And these groups would grow. They would not grow primarily as a consequence of the persuasive skill of their members to convince others to change their theology. They would grow because love of this sort, when it refuses to devolve into clannish exclusivity, is wildly contagious. And as they grew, the hearts in these familial communities would grow with them to accommodate a wider and wider horizon of love — to accommodate love of those within *and* beyond the growing community.

Jesus and Paul could help themselves to the concept of family to paint this picture of long-lasting and thoroughgoing devotion, investment, loyalty, and love for one another because it was simply assumed in that setting that families would exhibit the kinds of bonds they had in mind. They could assume the prior existence of that all-important context of the family for learning how to be truly human — to be a being-in-community. They needed only to encourage these families to walk into that second pregnancy — to learn that their hearts had been prepared for an expansion of love beyond their kin.

The Clarion call of Confucius to the West, I think, is that we in the West (many of us anyway) are not similarly situated. We've not learned to live well into that natural and God-given garden for the growth of the heart into an expansive love capable of taking in the neighbor, the enemy, and the world. And our Christian teachers are enjoining on us these expansive dimensions of Christian love without doing justice to the necessity of tending the garden — applying ourselves to the roots.

A caveat here is in order here to do justice to the occasional but very real need of Christian communities simply to *replace* families of origin as that garden from which one can first grow into an expansive heart of love. Some families of origin are so badly broken as to be incapable of functioning in the way that families are supposed to function. The Confucian call to renewed emphasis on filial piety should not be confused with a recommendation that anyone subject themselves to abuse or truly horrific circumstances. The church can and should offer to these unfortunate souls a place to start in their education toward expansive love. But it is not sustainable that this should be the norm. The very existence of a church that can function as a surrogate family presupposes a critical mass of practitioners living deeply into the relational dynamics of family. For any community to be an extension of healthy family relationships, there must be those (and not just a few) in the community who've lived well into the relationships that comprise family — family of the non-metaphorical sort. You cannot extend what you've not yet acquired.

And no family is perfect. So, were everyone with an imperfect family to forego the difficult work of learning filial piety in their family of origin in search of a surrogate family in the church, we'd likely lose our grip (as we have, in fact, lost our grip) on the power of filial piety thoroughly pursued. That means that many of us may owe it to our Christian communities to pursue the project of being a filial son or daughter more vigorously than we currently are. And for many of us, that's likely to be an awkward and painful business.

For some, a blunt reminder is in order that God is not your father. Your dad is your father. He's not perfect, of course. And his imperfections have very likely been a source of injury and pain for you. And there's a 50% chance that there are fathers out there who've done it better than has your father. You may need help and wise council to adjust your approach to him in the light of the particular injuries you've sustained from his imperfect parenting. But in the great mystery that is God's providence, your flesh-and-blood parents have been given to you in order for you to learn the dynamics of filial piety and submission appropriate to a son or daughter. Too often, the deep and significant metaphor of God-as-father is used as an excuse for neglecting the pursuit of that fundamental God-given relationship from within which to nourish the roots of goodness. We forget that the metaphor of God as father is, for all of its beauty and life-restoring power, a metaphor. And that it was never intended to supplant the opportunity to learn filial piety from relationship with our earthly parents. Many of us, I fear, owe it to ourselves and our Christian communities to approach our parents with renewed humility in order to explore afresh the opportunity for filial submission.

Encouraging typical Western Christians to be family together is a little bit like encouraging them to apply what they've learned about marathon running to their Christian life. Most have a vague idea about what goes into training for a marathon. And most have run some distance so they know (kind of) what running a marathon would be like. A small few have actually trained for and run marathons. And those folks are well-positioned to apply what they've learned to the Christian life. But most have never trained for or run a marathon. So they're just not very well positioned at all to extend the lessons of marathon-running to the Christian life. Similarly, I think the typical adult Western Christian has never pursued with much vigor the extended familial bonds that characterized the first-century Mediterranean family. So we're just not very well-positioned to take up the call of Jesus to extend the bonds characteristic of what he called "family" to our Christian communities. If that's true, we do well to heed the call of Confucius to vigorous pursuit of filial piety. In so doing, we'll be better positioned to heed the call of Jesus (and Confucius for that matter) to widen the heart beyond the family of origin.

Christians in the West, I think, find it very natural to suppose that growing as a Christian will make you a better father, spouse, son, etc. And, no doubt, there's some truth to the suggestion. Following Jesus certainly can't hurt in those areas. But reflection on the Confucian emphasis on filial piety can help us to appreciate the degree to which the reverse is true as well. Growing into a better son, father, sibling, and spouse will make you a better Christian. By tending the garden for the growth of these basic human relational dynamics, you'll position yourself to more fully live into the wider communal realities of the Way of Jesus. If the call of Jesus is a call to a deeply communal practice of his Way, and if the family is that natural and God-given venue for training in the relational dynamics of community, then you will be better positioned to practice the Way of Jesus to the degree that you've mastered the basic relational dynamics of family. When we apply ourselves to the roots, we ready ourselves for the expansion of the human heart so that it can embrace, not only our families, but our Christian brothers and sisters, our neighbors, our enemies, and the world.

CHAPTER 3

LEARNING

The Master said, "I will not open the door for a mind that is not already striving to understand, nor will I provide words to a tongue that is not already struggling to speak. If I hold up one corner of a problem, and the student cannot come back to me with the other three, I will not attempt to instruct him again."

ANALECTS 7.8

This is why I speak to them in parables, because seeing they do not see, and hearing they do not hear, nor do they understand.

MATTHEW 10:13

"JUST TELL ME!"

Silas is nearing the boiling point as he struggles through the "word-problems" section of his fourth-grade math homework. He's good at math; exceptional, in fact. But these, he insists, are *not* math problems. They're miniature stories clearly crafted with the intention of distracting frustrated fourth-graders from the problem to be solved by inundating them with trivial and irrelevant details. To solve this particular problem, the student must discern the area of a triangle from the given information about its sides. For Silas, that's a piece of cake. But he is not *told* to find the area of a triangle. What he's *told* is that Susan loves vine-ripened tomatoes. And that tomato seeds should be planted no less than 12 inches apart. And that Jim (who loves cucumbers) planted 7 cucumbers in a north-west line adjacent to the plot for Susan's tomato garden. And that cucumbers require no less than 15 inches between seeds. And myriad other facts that only distract from the work of discerning the area of triangles. Silas is begging me just to tell him what the *actual math problem* is that they want him to solve. He's not asking me to do the math for him. He's just asking me to sift through the meaningless dribble comprising the word-problem so that he can get down to the important work of practicing his math.

What's the point of word problems? Is the idea that math will be more entertaining, seemingly relevant, or otherwise pleasurable if couched in the language of everyday problem-solving? I doubt it. I'm certain that Silas is not the only fourth-grader for whom the word problems *detract* from the pleasure of doing math homework. Clearly educators have goals for these problems that go beyond practice in the ability to discern the area of a triangle given information about its sides. In fact, the frustration that Silas is feeling, it's tempting to suggest, is part of what is intended. There is a kind of growth that comes from wrestling with that stage that comes *before* mathematical calculation. In his previous math training, Silas had tasted something of the joy that comes with knowing how to complete a mathematical calculation. But he hadn't yet tasted the joy of progressing from un-certainty to certainty about the problem to be solved; the question to be answered.

I think the point of word problems (or, at least *a* point of word problems) is to begin to inculcate a love of learning. For many of us, learning is not something easily loved. The love of *knowledge* comes much easier to us. What's not to love about knowledge, after all? To know is to reach a kind of cognitive satisfaction, to achieve what Austrian philosopher Edmund Husserl called the "fulfillment" of what had been more or less empty intentions. To have knowledge is to have arrived. Beyond that, knowledge, as Francis Bacon so vividly insisted, is power. To know something is to have a kind of mastery over it. What is known can be predicted, manipulated, and sometimes controlled. Since the felt demand for knowledge is virtually universal, knowledge positions you to be a leader. If you know what others don't, and if they want to know what you know, then they'll follow you. If you know, you can instruct and exhort. Yours will be a weighty voice. So we love to know. And it takes very little training to love knowing. We love knowing because we love satisfaction, completion, power, and leadership. We love the rest that accompanies arrival.

Learning, on the other hand, is always incomplete. What you've mastered, what you know, you're no longer learning. To be learning is to be *in process.* It is to be on the way to knowledge. But it is not yet to have arrived. Your intentions toward the object of inquiry are still empty, unfulfilled. If you are learning, you do not have control, are not yet able to predict your subject matter. You are in the power-down position of dependency. You'll need to follow and submit to a teacher or to the demands of your subject matter if you're to make progress. To be learning is to be without the cognitive satisfaction and fulfillment — the rest that accompanies arrival — so characteristic of knowledge. To be learning is to feel the goal of knowledge frustrated and unachieved — even if only temporarily.

So it's no wonder that we require training if we're to fall in love with learning. While we're easily enamored of fulfillment, satisfaction, completion, power, and leadership, the opposite is true of incompletion, dependence, uncertainty, impotence, submission, and the power-down position of following. Humility is accidental, at best, to the love of knowledge. It is certainly possible to love and pursue knowledge from a position of humility. But you needn't be humble to love knowledge. And, as we all know both from our own experience and from the Apostle Paul, knowledge is often accompanied by quite the opposite condition. To know is to be in danger of "puffing up" — to be at risk of thinking too highly of yourself. The love of learning, on the other hand, *requires* the love of humility. You cannot love to be in the position of the learner without some degree of love for humble submission.

Knowledge is, of course, extremely important. Without it, we cannot be appropriately responsive to our world. So it's no shortcoming of the human condition that we're so naturally enamored of knowledge. But, caught up as we are in this love affair with knowledge that so naturally characterizes our cognitive endeavors, it's easy to lose sight of the value of learning — easy never to fall in love with learning. We'll *put up* with learning, perhaps, because it's what's required to get what we *really* want, which is knowledge. But learning will be, for us, like going to the dentist. I hate the dentist. Nevertheless, I pay exorbitant costs for the privilege of sitting in his chair because I hate poor dental health even more. For some, learning is like that. They hate it. But they'll put up with it — maybe even pay exorbitant costs to acquire it — because they hate something else even more — ignorance. The thing of primary concern is knowledge. For them learning is valuable only insofar as it contributes to the cognitive goal of knowing.

For the Confucian, on the other hand, these priorities are reversed. A life characterized by continual learning is the thing most to be valued. Knowledge, as attractive and important as it is, is simply the byproduct of having fallen in love with and pursued that thing which is of first importance — a life of learning. This reversal of priorities finds its expression in pedagogy. If what you prize above all is knowledge, you'll elevate an approach to teaching that emphasizes clear, unambiguous, and (so far as possible) exhaustive articulation of the truth. The student's job will be to internalize and stand ready to recapitulate the truths taught. The capacity to recapitulate will be the primary indication that learning has been achieved.

Where the goal is to inculcate a love for the incompleteness and submission characteristic of learning, however, teaching takes a different form. Maximally clear articulation of the truth gives way to mind-bending paradox. Exhaustive presentation of the subject matter gives way to cryptic aphorism. And the ability to recapitulate gives way to the capacity to fill in what is missing as the primary indication that learning is being achieved. Insofar as we've fallen in love with knowledge but not learning, the cryptic and paradoxical wisdom characteristic of the Confucian *Analects* will be nothing but frustrating. "Just tell me!" we'll think as we wrestle with the one corner of the problem presented in the text. We'll demand that Confucius hold up all four corners. But he'll give us just the one because his primary aim is not to deliver up once for all the information to be mastered and recapitulated. Instead, the master's aim is to guide us into those conversations and thought experiments out of which will arise a gradual filling out of the corners. Increasing knowledge will likely be the result. And that's to be celebrated, of course. But the master's primary aim is to initiate learning — to set the student searching in a particular direction and in such a way as to make possible for the student the gradual overcoming of ignorance.

Imagine, then, what it would be like to have positive affection for learning. Does your heart leap at the thought of being impotent? Submissive? At the thought of incomplete inquiry? Do you find yourself hoping and praying that your kids will find their way into friendships and social circumstances at school where they are the followers? Do you relish the opportunity to depend on someone or something else? Do you revel in the frustration (even if temporary) of that cognitive goal of arrival — of knowledge? If not, then reflection on the Confucian emphasis on love of learning may afford you the opportunity to recapture a deep human good.

But are these things — impotence, uncertainty, submission, dependency — really things to be celebrated, loved, and sought? Do we *want* to learn from Confucius to have positive affection for these conditions — to seek them for ourselves and to wish them upon our children? Perhaps a sober assessment of my life will affect a kind of *resignation* to the unavoidable fact that I'll experience impotence, submission, dependency, and the like. But are we really supposed to *like* these things?

For the Christian, the answer to that question is a resounding Yes. When God created Adam, he built into the very fabric of his being precisely these conditions. Adam was designed for inclusion in a community wherein he would eternally be the follower. In the context of the community for which he was created, Adam was *designed to be* eternally — inescapably — in the power-down position. He was designed to be relatively impotent, submissive, dependent, unknowing — to be the follower. Forever. And it was the being of this power-down-by-design creature that was declared good by his creator. God liked it.

But at the center of the fall, then and now, is a profound disenchantment with the power-down condition built into the fabric of human nature. We've fallen out of love with what God designed us to be. Our obsession with knowledge has blinded us to the beauty of unknowing, impotence, submission, and dependence. Perhaps reflecting on the Confucian emphasis on the love of learning can help us find our way back.

Last summer, Laurel and I celebrated God's gift of twenty years of marriage together. In comparison with the way we know each other now, we were virtual strangers on that magical day when we made our lives one. It's been twenty beautiful years of mutual discovery. Deep recesses of personality and character have slowly, over time, made their way into our collective consciousness. With increasing accuracy over the years, I've found myself capable of predicting her thoughts, reactions, behaviors, and feelings. And she mine. And it's a beautiful thing. Our increasing knowledge of the other has allowed us to move more and more fully into an approximation of that beautiful ideal of being fully known *and* fully accepted. To know and to be known by Laurel is one of the deepest joys of my life.

But we're still learning and, occasionally, I still experience the frustration characteristic of the learning process. In those moments, Laurel is a mystery to me. I can't find my way into her perspective — can't predict or understand her reactions. I can't find any genuine sympathy for the way she's feeling. I am reminded that we're still learning about one another. For all of my progress toward understanding, there is still much about Laurel that I *don't* know. I'm the learner. And I'm powerless to learn without her willingness to explore with me. If I'm going to continue to learn, I'll need to follow her lead — to submit to her instruction. I am impotent, uncertain, submissive, and dependent. To think otherwise is to succumb to the illusion that people can be known — deeply known — whether or not they want to be. If I'm going to continue to make progress in my discovery of the beautifully complex person with whom God gave it to me to share a life, I'll need her cooperation. She'll need to lead the way.

And I love it. I wouldn't have it any other way.

Suppose God appeared one day in our living room and plopped the "Knowledge Button" down on our living room table. Suppose He told us that we could, if we both wanted to, push the button together resulting in our having complete and exhaustive knowledge of one another. In an instant, we could know everything about each other that it is possible for another person to know. No more mystery. No more frustrating nights spent in tears trying without success to grasp the perspective of the other. No more failed predictions. No more disappointed expectations. Suppose God gave *you* that opportunity with a person in your life with whom it has been given you to enjoy increasingly deep love. Would you push the button?

I wouldn't. Not for all the money in the world. It's not because there are things about me that I wish to keep hidden from Laurel. And it's not because I think there are things about her that I'd rather not know. My deep desire is to progress in our knowledge of one another so that on our 40th anniversary, it will be tempting to say that we hardly knew each other at all when we celebrated our 20th. For as long as God gives us to be together, I hope with all my being to make progress toward full and exhaustive knowledge of one another.

But I don't want to arrive.

It's a strange and paradoxical feeling. I rejoice with every step along the path toward exhaustive knowledge. Each step has as a consequence that there's one less occasion for tearful impotence to understand or to achieve sympathy for Laurel's perspective. It's a step in the direction of that unity of mind and spirit for which we strive. And it's wonderful. But I recoil at the thought of taking the *final* step. As much as I love knowing Laurel, I love something else just as much — maybe more. I love learning about her. And I love helping her to learn about me. I love the life-long process of mutual discovery. I love *finding out* as much as I love *knowing*. Something of inestimable value would be lost to me were Laurel and I to find ourselves suddenly (or even not so suddenly) at the *end* of our life-long journey of mutual discovery. Lost would be the joy of finding out, the periodic overcoming of frustrated attempts to know. The thought that we had, for the very last time, experienced that deep soul sigh of relief that comes with *finally* getting it after a long struggle to understand would be, for me, a deeply sad one.

So I embrace the impotence, uncertainty, and submission that are required to be in the process of *finding out*. I embrace these things not merely for the knowledge I can acquire thereby. I embrace them as part of the essence of this deeply good journey that is my marriage to Laurel. I embrace them as essential components of this unfolding thing that is our love for one another. And I'd not trade them for all the knowledge in the world.

This realization that love resists comprehensive knowledge of the other may give us a window through which to catch a glimpse of the divine judgment that Adam was good. He was not good *despite* his impotence, dependence, and unknowing. He was designed to be that way. And the design plan was a good one. It was good, in part, because it made possible for Adam those dimensions of love that require the possibility of discovery and learning.

For all of his enthusiasm for learning, though, Confucius also recognized the importance of knowledge. Not only does knowledge make appropriate response to our world possible, it is that essential foundation from which learning can be responsibly pursued. Knowledge represents a kind of completion. It is the fulfillment of the cognitive quest. It is knowledge, then, that has the ability to provide stability for the incomplete, unfulfilled, and messy business of learning. Confucius worried about his students who, in their enthusiasm for progress and fresh thinking, had failed to retain the knowledge that had been passed on to them by the ancients. These were the "wild scholars." In their enthusiasm for new learning, they were in danger of drifting anchorless and untethered to the hard-won knowledge of those who had gone before. They loved to *think*. But they did not allow their thought to be constrained by knowledge previously won. Without the foundation of that secure knowledge, their thinking was reckless and dangerous.

On the other hand, Confucius was convinced that secure knowledge safely handed down from the past, if not accompanied by fresh and critical thought, was useless. As much as he worried about his reckless students, the wild scholars, he preferred their posture to that of the "fastidious scholars." The fastidious scholars could recite eloquently the deliverances of the ancients, but they refused to "get their hands dirty" with the business of fresh, creative, or critical thinking. Their fear of any deviation from the past halted the creative process necessary to render that knowledge relevant and useful in context. As a result, their knowledge was increasingly dispassionate and detached from the realities of everyday life.

A well-ordered love of learning, according to Confucius, steers a middle path between the wild and the fastidious scholar. It respects the authority of secured knowledge handed down from the past. But it recognizes the need for fresh thinking and new perspectives if that knowledge is to find expression, articulation, and useful application in any particular context. Wisdom requires the ability to discern in which direction you're more likely steering and to make corrections in the direction of the opposite error. To find the middle, those erring in the direction of the wild are encouraged to move in the direction of the fastidious and vice versa.

If you're not sure which error is the more likely one for you, then wisdom would have you to direct your efforts to the avoidance of the more pernicious of the two errors — that of fastidiousness. The wild scholar, though reckless and dangerous, is nevertheless operating from that deep impulse that drives the well-ordered love of learning — the desire to make progress in thought in order to *live* well. Fastidiousness is the more pernicious of the two errors because it threatens to divorce knowledge from life. Confucius repeatedly warns against confusing increasing eloquence in the articulation of secured knowledge with learning. This error is dangerous because it conduces so easily to this confusion. It threatens to replace the art of living well with the art of eloquent articulation as the end of learning.

Anyone who has lived in Christian community will recognize this tension. Wild Christians, caught up in their love of relevance, praxis, and fresh thinking, risk fracturing that rich trans-temporal, trans-generational community that is the body of Christ through the ages. They're the more likely to scorn the creeds or to downplay the preservation of traditional orthodoxy and doctrine. They're the more likely to forget that creeds afford the body of Christ a place to stand *together* throughout the generations. When I recite the creeds, I lock arms with my ancestors in the faith. I internalize my solidarity with them. I am not alone. To scorn the creeds is to float anchorless in a sea of ideas — a reckless and dangerous condition even if it *does* turn up an exciting new perspective here and there. Fastidious Christians, on the other hand, caught up in their love of secure knowledge, risk the uselessness of irrelevant (even if orthodox) doctrine and the praise of eloquence.

For all of their differences, though, the wild and the fastidious have in common a failure to love learning. Recall that the position of the learner is submissive and unknowing. To be a learner is to be a follower. To embrace learning is to embrace incompletion.

To be wild is to have embraced unknowing and uncertainty. The wild scholar likely thrills at the thought of the not-yet-discovered. The incompleteness of our knowledge of God and his way with the world excites and draws. She would suffer something like disappointment were she to learn that she'd finally discovered the very last thing of much significance that there was to discover about God and his way with the world. A god for whom that was a possibility would be, somehow, too small a god.

But the wild scorn the submissive posture of following at the heart of the well-ordered love of learning. They *do not* thrill at the thought of there being an authoritative collection of ideas to function as a foundation and a constraint on creative expression and inquiry. They spend little if any time in pursuit of the art of faithful conformity. They've succumbed in their thinking to the siren's call of uniqueness that rings so loudly in the ears of contemporary Western culture. Prized is the opportunity to say something *new* — to be a *leader.*

Perhaps more than anything else, the contemporary obsession with leadership fuels the error in the direction of the wild. Somehow we've come to think that there is something intrinsically good about positions of leadership — that life is somehow better from that position. We spend untold energy in the attempt to unearth the secrets to being a leader — the skills that must be developed in order to ascend to that coveted position. We assume that following is just what happens by default if you aren't lucky enough to be the leader. Lost is the suggestion that following is an art — that there are secrets to following well and that the highest dimensions of human fulfillment might be achievable precisely from the position of the follower. We forget that at the center of the Christian Way is the invitation to be a follower. Conformity is the very heart of Christian discipleship. Leadership, if and when it happens, is accidental to the Way of Jesus. Everyone is called to be a follower. Whether or not we find ourselves in positions of leadership, it is our ability to follow that will dictate our success as disciples.

For the wild, conformity and the position of the follower have given way to the cult of leadership and the thrill of novelty. They would sooner read a book detailing practices aimed at the development of leadership skills than one detailing practices aimed at thriving as a follower or the skills required to conform in one's thinking to the thought of another. The wild Christian needs reminding that Jesus himself retained the posture of the follower. His leadership, such as it was, issued from a more basic posture of submissive conformity to the will of his Father and to the Way articulated in the law and prophets. Wild Christians fail to love learning because they fail to love the submissive posture of the follower. They hate conformity. And without conformity there can be no learning. To learn anything is to conform the mind to that which is learned or to the person from whom one is learning.

To be fastidious, on the other hand, is to have embraced the submission and conformity requisite for a well-ordered love of learning. The fastidious prize authority. They're quick to accuse the wild Christians of failing to take seriously the authority of scripture and the wisdom of orthodoxy handed down through the creeds. They thrill at the thought of a seamless and unbroken chain of conformity stretching from their own carefully-articulated affirmations back through the creeds to the very teachings of Jesus and the apostles. The thought of breaking with the traditionally affirmed for the sake of something new, interesting, or seemingly more relevant holds little if any appeal. They'll hesitate and request a fair bit of qualification before acceding to the suggestion that "open-mindedness" is a virtue.

But the fastidious scorn the love of unknowing, the embrace of mystery and uncertainty, that lies at the heart of the well-ordered love of learning. They've succumbed to a love of knowledge that *precludes* the love of learning. They don't want to dirty their hands with fresh new thinking that may take them afield of traditional affirmations. Like the tragic fellow Jesus describes as having cut off his limbs so that he could rest in the safe assurance that he would do nothing wrong, the fastidious cut themselves off from any novel source of wisdom so that they can rest in the safe assurance that they're not *thinking* anything wrong. They'll be far slower than their wild brothers and sisters to recognize the value of seeking wisdom from sources other than the scriptures and the traditional affirmations of the church. The idea that what has been handed down is *incomplete* in any significant way will not thrill but offend.

The fastidious are the most likely in need of reminding that the ability to eloquently articulate the deliverances of orthodoxy is no predictor of Christian maturity. They would do well to learn from that star pupil of Confucius, Zilu. When Zilu learned something new, but had not yet been able to put it into practice, his only fear was that he would learn another new thing. The fastidious need reminding that affirmation in conformity with orthodoxy is not the end game. Orthodoxy is only as good as its capacity to facilitate a life of Jesus-following.

To love learning is to embrace unknowing, uncertainty, incompleteness, impotence, and the submissive posture of the follower. The wild embrace unknowing and uncertainty but scorn the submissive and impotent posture of the follower. The fastidious embrace the submissive posture of the follower but scorn the embrace of uncertainty, mystery, and incompleteness. A well-ordered love of learning is neither wild nor fastidious. How do we steer the course between these two very different failures to love learning?

The first step, recall, is to discern which for you is the more tempting of the two errors. If you love uncertainty and discovery but grimace at the thought of conformity and submission to authority, you're likely to err most naturally in the direction of the wild. If your thinking is risk-averse, if you revel in your conformity with orthodoxy and recoil at the thought that what has been handed down is in any significant way incomplete, you're more likely to be among the fastidious. If you're not sure in which direction you tend to err, ask someone with whom you've recently had a theological disagreement. They'll likely be in a fairly good position to tell you.

If you suspect that you're among the fastidious, a good first step might be to find a few people that you consider to be sincere — even if wild — followers of Jesus. Ask them if they'd be willing to explore sources of wisdom other than those handed down from your tradition. In the spirit of this book, you might try to put together a group of Christians with whom to read through the *Analects* of Confucius together. Read them not in order to point out all of the similarities and differences with traditional orthodox Christian thought. Read them as scientists of human flourishing. Read them in search of anything that might conduce to the human life well-lived. Remember that Jesus loves you. And he wants you to flourish. And he would have you to find ideas conducive to your flourishing wherever they are to be found. He won't be threatened in the slightest if you find ideas conducive to your flourishing somewhere other than in his teachings or the teachings of his followers.

If you suspect that you're among the wild, a good first step might be to find a few people that you consider to be sincere — even if fastidious — followers of Jesus. Ask them if they'd be willing to explore the history of Christian creedal affirmation with you. You might even experiment with memorizing some of the classical creedal affirmations of the Christian faith. Experiment with studying the creeds *in order to* submit to them. Do not approach them as just fascinating history of the tradition with which you identify. Engage them as authorities. Experiment with the attempt to conform your thought to theirs. Endeavor to harmonize what you know from other sources (science, psychology, the humanities, history, whatever) with what has been affirmed through the ages by the masters of the Christian life.

If you're not sure whether you're wild or fastidious, even after asking someone with whom you've recently had a theological disagreement, then work at avoiding the more pernicious of the two errors, that of fastidiousness. Most of the Christians with whom I live have got a better acquaintance with the scriptures and the basic contours of Christian orthodoxy than most Christians who've ever lived. Many of us have filled our heads with Christian orthodoxy far more quickly than we've been able to figure out how to live into the knowledge we've acquired. Perhaps we would do well to learn from Zilu. We would do well to assiduously avoid the acquisition of new information until we've made some progress in the direction of practicing those things we've already learned. Some of our churches, I think, would do well to cancel sermons for a year in order to give 40 minutes each week to the practice of what has already been eloquently articulated — over and over again.

The point of word problems, I think, is at least twofold: First, it is to give fourth graders that wonderful experience of *transition* from frustrated unknowing impotence to the satisfying fulfillment of knowledge. You cannot have *that* transition without living through the frustrated lack of fulfillment embodied in its first stage. To love learning, we must learn to love and embrace its earliest stages. Otherwise we'll lose sight of the beauty of learning in our love affair with its fruit, the fulfillment of knowledge. Equally important, though, is the project of reinforcing confidence in the relevance of math. For those unimpressed by the intrinsic beauty of those algorithms that allow for the discerning of the area of triangles, there is the need for learning through experience that those algorithms will help us to grow better cucumbers — that knowing the algorithms conduces to the good life. And for those who could very happily work with algorithms all day long, there is the needed reminder that the garden needs to be tended and that our algorithms, as intrinsically beautiful as they are, have work to do.

CHAPTER 4

ETHICS

Someone asked, "What do you think of the saying, 'Requite injury with kindness'?" The Master replied, "With what, then, would one requite kindness? Requite injury with uprightness, and kindness with kindness."

ANALECTS 14.34

You have heard that it was said, "You shall love your neighbor and hate your enemy. But I say to you, love your enemies and pray for those who persecute you so that you may be sons of your Father who is in heaven; for He causes His sun to rise on the evil and the good, and sends rain on the righteous and the unrighteous.

MATT. 5: 43-45

Enemy Love

"I REGRET NOW," SAID Abbe Faria, "having helped you in your late inquiries or having given you the information that I did." "Why so?" inquired Dantes.

"Because it has instilled a new passion in your heart — that of vengeance."

Dumas' crazy priest recognizes, in this prophetic moment, that by making clear to Dantes the true explanation of his misfortune, he has given birth to the Count of Monte Cristo. He has set in motion a vengeance-inspired course that will be a force for ill both in those upon whom vengeance is being affected and in the agent of that vengeance himself.

Still, I'm conflicted. Something in me roots for the Count. I want justice to rain down on these men who've ruined his life. And it's not just that I want them to pay for their crimes. I want justice to come at the hand of the one who has been wronged. Even as I see the bent for vengeance twisting Dantes' soul, I want him to stay the course — to finish what he has started. I want him to achieve the satisfaction of perfectly executed vengeance. And I want this *for his sake,* even as the plot makes it increasingly clear that revenge won't bring the satisfaction he seeks.

What does virtue require in the face of injury and opposition? How ought I to be postured toward my enemy? How should I respond? And how would I feel about my enemy if I were a person of admirable character? The great religious leaders and moralists in recorded history have been virtually unanimous in their rejection of a respond-in-kind approach to injury and opposition. They've known that Dantes' course is not the way of virtue. They've encouraged us to resist the temptation to think that vengeance will satisfy our longings for justice.

So suppose I've resolved not to respond in kind (or at least to endeavor so not to respond). Still, I might wonder, how should I be? Are there specific affects, postures, and behaviors characteristic of the moral hero in the context of injury and opposition? If so, what are they?

A tempting response comes to us from the Taoist stream of thought in classical Chinese philosophy. According to the Taoist masters, the person of virtue has a character so firmly established that her response to others is unaffected by the way she is treated. Her postures toward others are the same for all. Her ways of being with and treating other people are entirely fixed by the inner state of her heart and mind. Were you only to observe her behavior and attitudes, you would have no clue as to whether the person with whom she is interacting is friend or foe. She is a picture of stability and consistency. She has a single set of dispositions (summed up with the word "kindness") toward everyone with whom she has any interaction. The Taoist would urge on Dantes a response to his oppressors that is unconditioned by the atrocities of their behavior toward him. Were he a person of virtue and strength, he would treat them in just the way he would treat anyone else — including his friends.

And isn't this exactly what Jesus teaches? Jesus encourages his followers to love their enemies and to pray for those who persecute them. Isn't this exactly what we should be doing for our friends? Surely we should love and pray for everyone. So you might think the teachings of Jesus to include the suggestion that there should be no difference in your approach to friends and enemies. In fact, for a model of appropriate response to enemies, Jesus points to the Heavenly Father's equal treatment of the righteous and the wicked — he sends his rain on both as a blessing. Moreover, he criticizes the one who loves and greets only his brother suggesting that his followers ought to meet opposition with these same attitudes (Matt. 5:46-47). The hero of one of his most popular stories is a Samaritan who treats a would-be enemy in just the way that one would ordinarily treat a friend. He rescues him and is proactive in pursuit of his flourishing.

It's for reasons like these that many (including many who've never heard of Taoism or any of the Taoist masters) are tempted to read Jesus as though his was the Taoist line on the proper treatment of enemies. To be like Jesus, it is thought, is to treat everyone the same — friend or enemy. It is to be a person of such inner strength (or connection to God) that one's behaviors and postures toward the other are utterly unaffected by the attitudes, behaviors, and postures of the other. It is to approximate God's treatment of us — conditioned only by His perfectly loving and perfectly fixed character.

Confucius, on the other hand, was set squarely against this Taoist stream of thought. When asked whether we should respond with kindness to injury, the master rhetorically asks how then we would respond to kindness. The point of this passage in the *Analects* is to invite reflection on the chaos that would be the result of responding in like manner to everyone and everything that comes our way.

According to the Confucian way, the good person is able to discern even very subtle dimensions of her relational environment and to respond appropriately *in context*. There is no fixed pattern of behavior and attitude characteristic of the good person in every circumstance. The good person will discern, among other things, the nature of the relationships involved in any particular situation. Her response to the other will be appropriately flexible. Is the person with whom I am interacting my superior? My brother? My parent? Am I the mother in this situation? The co-worker? The employee? The employer? The teacher? The student? Is the person to whom I am responding a friend? An enemy? A stranger? A mere acquaintance? Is it someone indebted to me somehow? Or is it someone to whom I am in debt? How is power distributed in this circumstance? And who else will be affected by my behaviors and postures (either as observers or as people directly affected by my actions)? Am I father to them? Brother? And so on.

To the Confucian mind, there is no single pattern of response that is appropriate regardless of these and countless other (sometimes quite subtle) variations in one's relational context. It invites confusion and chaos to suggest that there is. In human interactions — as everywhere — order is a result of wise and proper discrimination. There is an order in the context of human relationships that fits various encounters and relational dynamics with appropriate responses (or ranges of appropriate response). To have settled on a single response for everyone regardless of the relational dynamics in play is to have denied the existence of this order and to have invited chaos. The sage determines the types of relationship in play and responds with the behaviors and attitudes properly associated with his position in those particular relationships. The response of the good person, then, will depend *both* upon the well-formed character of her heart *and* upon the relational specifics of her particular situation.

So, in response to kindness, the good person recognizes the value of reciprocity and responds with kindness. But reciprocity is ill-suited to govern good behavior in the context of injury. In the context of injury, the good person is upright. To demand that one's response be insensitive to the relational dynamics in play is to do violence to the very real value of reciprocity. A policy of kindness to all renders kindness incapable of manifesting the good of reciprocity. It's no longer *reciprocal* kindness if one would have been kind come what may. Perhaps there is some very general category of response — like uprightness — that is appropriate to any circumstances. One should be upright. Always. But specific manifestations of uprightness, like kindness, will not always be a good fit for the relational dynamics in play. Or so argued Confucius, anyway.

With the Confucian emphasis on flexibility and sensitivity to relational dynamics in view, let us revisit Jesus. Did Jesus teach that the response of the good person is blind to the relational dynamics of the situation? No. Jesus taught that our response to enemies and friends should have these things in common: We should pray for, love, and bless our enemies and friends alike. But that leaves room for significant variation in our response to enemies and friends.

And a moment's reflection is all it takes to realize that Jesus did not respond in the same way to everyone with whom he interacted. He, like the Confucian sage (and in opposition to the wisdom of Taoism) was sensitive to relational dynamics in his dealings with others. Nowhere does he teach that one's response to everyone — friend, foe, brother, sister, father, stranger, student, teacher — should be the same. Rather, in the teachings of Jesus one finds varying instructions for the complex array of interpersonal relations — instructions sensitive to the dynamics unique to the *kind* of relationship being addressed. Children are to respect and honor parents but not *vice versa* (at least not in the same way). The student is to be in subjection to the Master. Jesus himself lived a life of submission to the father, but not to his disciples. So there is no reason to think that Jesus would have settled on a single complete set of behaviors and attitudes appropriate in the context of friend and foe.

So suppose I've endeavored to love, bless, and pray for my enemy. Still my way of being with them might differ significantly from my way of being with friends. I may admire, trust, seek to imitate, congratulate, and bestow praise upon my friend. On the other hand, I may pity, seek to differentiate myself from, sternly exhort, distrust, and defend against my enemy — all the while praying for, blessing, and loving him.

What's more, Jesus did not respond indiscriminately to friend and foe. Consider the difference between his treatment of his disciples and friends and his treatment of the religious leaders of the day who opposed and sought to injure him. His response to opposition is shot through with biting sarcasm (sometimes with the result that they were publicly humiliated), sharp accusation, and purposeful obscurity. Still, he presumably loved them, prayed for them, and genuinely desired and sought after their good. His posture toward his disciples and friends is palpably different. He is gentle, patient to explain, forgiving of error, and sympathetic. Even the most cursory survey of the life he lived in the presence of others belies the suggestion that he endorsed a view according to which one's response to the other should be insensitive to the distinction between friend and foe. What he *does* teach is that response to friend and foe alike should arise out of a condition of love, prayer for, and genuine pursuit of the good of the other.

But why, one wonders, is there so much emphasis on flexibility in the Confucian tradition and so much emphasis on impartiality in the teachings of Jesus? Why does Jesus so often sound as though he's endorsing a Taoist line according to which we ought to treat everyone the same way? Isn't this an indication of some kind of tension between the Confucian trajectory and the Christian trajectory when it comes to response to injury and opposition?

Reconciling the differing trajectories of these two teachers requires attention to the error to which each was responding. Confucius was responding to the Taoist approach to the good life according to which one's behavior should flow entirely out of one's character — that it should not be conditioned on circumstances and the relational dynamics of one's environment. Confucius was at pains to emphasize the importance of flexibility, sensitivity to context, and relational dynamics.

Jesus, on the other hand, was responding to what James calls "the sin of partiality." Apparently, it was thought in Jesus' context that folks were deserving of different degrees of inclusion, acceptance, respect, and good treatment depending on where they stood with respect to several key distinctions; chief among them, the following: Jew/ Gentile, male/female, slave/free, rich/poor, healthy/sick. Jesus was at pains to emphasize the importance of a life of love and blessing without regard for these and other distinctions.

So Confucius emphasized the degree to which the response of the good person will vary with circumstance. Jesus emphasized the dimensions along which the response of the good person will be blind to distinctions that are sometimes thought to be of significance. But neither adopts a respond-in-kind approach to injury and opposition. And, closer to the point at hand, neither endorses a Taoist line according to which the good person is insensitive to the relational dynamics of her particular circumstances.

The Demands of Morality

The Taoist attempt to isolate goodness from the particulars of circumstance is one manifestation of an approach to morality that is widely adopted by morally serious people (Taoists and otherwise). It's an enticing thought that the good person could be understood, or perhaps even described or defined, apart from the particulars of her unique circumstances. For those who take the moral life seriously, it's hard to resist the attempt to codify the demands of morality — to lay down once and for all the rules that govern the behaviors and attitudes of the good person in any and every circumstance.

In his mid-forties, it occurred to Ethan that he couldn't remember a season in his life when he consistently tithed. He'd been a Christian all his life and had, just in recent years, found his way into something approximating financial stability. So he'd been feeling guilty about his failure to tithe. He believed in the authority of the Bible and had a (rather vague) notion that biblical stewardship of resources includes a regular practice of tithing so he made the decision to tithe. But then he wondered:

Before or after taxes?

The difference would be significant given Ethan's expenses and other commitments. He asked his pastor. His pastor gave him the happy news that the taxes withheld from his paycheck are never *really* his to begin with. He needs only tithe on those resources over which he has real discretion. Real stewardship. Whew!

So Ethan tithed regularly for three or four years. It was tough at first. But five or six months into his new practice, he (wisely) set things up in such a way that the money came out of his paycheck automatically and went directly to the church. He never saw the money. Never had to think about it. Didn't have to wrestle every month with the decision whether or not to write the check. And he experienced the joy that comes from the often hard-won belief that one is doing the right thing — satisfying the demands of morality. He was living biblically (at least insofar as the stewardship of his resources were concerned).

Then the roof caved in. Ethan's neighbor and friend lost his job and found himself in danger of losing his home in the middle-class neighborhood in which Ethan lived. With the money he was tithing to his church, Ethan could give his neighbor some relief from the distress of his circumstances. But he couldn't tithe *and* help his neighbor without seriously altering his lifestyle (e.g., firing his gardener, canceling his cable TV service, and trading in his new-ish Honda for a an old beater functioning just well enough to get him to work and back).

Ethan went back to his pastor. Can I stop tithing to help my neighbor?

The answer this time was not so encouraging. "Tithes are one thing," said his pastor. "Offerings are another." What biblical steward-ship requires is that you continue your tithe come what may. Beyond that, Jesus calls us to a life of generosity to neighbor. His pastor en-couraged Ethan to continue his tithe and to consider giving gener-ously to his neighbor.

Ethan fired his gardener who, unbeknownst to Ethan because Ethan never talked to him, was losing business left and right due to a failing economy. He cancelled his cable service, and bought an old jalopy. He began subsidizing his neighbor's mortgage payment with the money he was saving. He kept his tithe intact.

This went on for several months. And Ethan, once again, expe-rienced the satisfaction of doing the right thing. But as the months wore on and his neighbor remained jobless, he wondered if he was in fact doing the right thing. The urgency with which his neighbor pursued work seemed to be waning. His church spent a million dol-lars updating its facilities. He heard through the grapevine that his gardener was out of work, had been evicted from his apartment, and was barely off the streets — living month to month in a low-cost motel in a neighboring city.

At the same time, Ethan made some new Christians friends. These were folks who thought that the contemporary Christian obsession with "tithing" was wrong-headed. Rather, they claimed, one should be "justice minded" with regard to one's resources. They encouraged Ethan to discontinue his tithe — to stop contributing to the enter-tainment of well-to-do Christians that was the weekly Sunday ser-vice at his church. They acquainted Ethan with the horrific suffering endured needlessly by victims of injustice around the globe. They encouraged Ethan to sell his gas-guzzling jalopy and buy a far more expensive hybrid, to alter his eating habits in such a way as not to be complicit in the needless suffering of animals and to stop watering his lawn. They encouraged Ethan to live simply, which he endeavored to do. But then Ethan wondered:

"How simple is simple enough?"

He never could get a straight answer to that question. On the one hand, it seemed that it would never be simple enough unless he was teetering on the edge of financial disaster himself. On the other hand, he was encouraged to take some comfort from the idea that he was driving a hybrid and growing succulents instead of grass.

What should we say about Ethan? Is he moving in the right direction? One thing seems certain. Ethan seems more concerned with discovering and living up to the demands of morality than he does with loving those with whom he has effective contact. This is not to say that he's unloving. He feels deeply for and loves the people with whom he has regular interaction. But his attempts at moral seriousness seem strangely disconnected from the love that he feels for those with whom he lives and among whom he moves. His moral seriousness takes the form of a longing for answers to questions like these:

Should one tithe come what may?

Should one spend more money on a car in order to drive a hybrid?

Should one help one's neighbor stay in his expensive house when folks elsewhere are without shelter of any kind?

If one makes $120,000 per year, how much exactly (or even roughly) can one keep for oneself?

With answers to enough questions like these, he could (quite apart from *being* in any particular circumstance) discern what morality would require of *anyone* in *any* particular circumstance. And he longs for the satisfaction of knowing that he's satisfied the demands of morality. This is what drives him.

And insofar as he's come to be convinced that the Bible is our best source of information about morality, he'll be on the lookout for answers to questions like these in the Bible. He'll look to Jesus, for example, for the rules that govern appropriate behavior and attitudes in any circumstances whatever. He'll attempt to extract principles from the teachings of Jesus like the following:

> *So long as one tithes, one may do whatever one wishes with the rest of one's income.*

> *One must divest oneself of material possessions until one reaches the level of bare subsistence, at which point one may be satisfied that one's life is sufficiently simple.*

> *One must give to those circumstances in one's acquaintance that are most dire.*

> *One must not grow a lawn if it can be established that growing succulents where one lives is easier on the planet.*

> *One must give to those people living closest to one even if their circumstances are not most dire.*

The Confucian way will have none of this. Goodness, for the Confucian, is a matter of discerning the complex dynamics of one's particular circumstance and acting appropriately. But the dynamics of *any* particular circumstance are staggeringly complex. Every morally significant decision takes place in the context of a particular history with particular people. No two situations are exactly alike. So to attempt the articulation of rules that would govern behavior in any and every circumstance is to chase a pipe dream. And to seek the satisfaction of living in accordance with such rules is, likewise, to chase after something that cannot be attained (or can be attained only by dint of some degree of self-deception).

One becomes good not by identifying those rules that govern goodness in any and every circumstance, but by following and imitating one who is already good; by subjecting and submitting oneself to a master of the good life.

The Confucian who approaches Jesus will not find it at all natural to search for and extract from his teachings the kind of code — the kinds of rules — for which Ethan longs. So it will be no surprise to the morally serious Confucian that one searches in vain for anything like a satisfactory list of universally applicable rules in the teachings of Jesus. In fact, Jesus seems altogether unconcerned with providing such a thing. Rather, he invites his disciples to follow him into the nitty-gritty circumstances of life in his time where his behavior is, one must say, sometimes really quite surprising and unpredictable. He tells stories that illustrate the condition of the good and bad heart. But he does not seem terribly interested in the project of articulating anything like a completed moral code (either a code of conduct or a code of the heart, whatever that would be). On the other hand, as a consequence of his moral instruction, there arose a team of personally powerful and morally courageous practitioners of his Way. There arose the Church.

Along the way, Jesus addresses the manifestation in Israel of the attempt to be morally serious by means of ever-increasing specificity concerning the demands of morality (in his context, the

Law) — the attempt to articulate the demands of goodness from a position that transcends the uniqueness of any particular life. The religious leaders of that time were, to put it mildly, morally serious folk. And they had adopted an attempt to be increasingly specific about the Law's requirements as a strategy for being serious about the execution of the Law. Jesus saw this for the dead end that it was and taught his disciples that unless they move beyond the righteousness of the Scribes and Pharisees, they would miss out on his Way. This does not require heaping additional moral rules on their already-impressive list (perhaps even adding a list of rules for the "heart" to the existing rules that govern "mere behavior"). Rather, to go beyond the righteousness of the scribes and Pharisees is to reject their strategy for being serious about the requirements of the law — to reject the articulation of increasingly specific principles or rules capable of dictating behavior and attitudes for any and all circumstances.

I, for one, have spent more time than I care to admit trying to extract principles from Jesus' teachings that would yield answers to questions like Ethan's. And I've found it futile and frustrating. Reflection on the Confucian insistence on context sensitivity and the impossibility of articulating the demands of goodness by means of abstract principles has opened up for me the possibility that I've been trying to extract something that Jesus never intended to communicate.

This is not to say that the Confucian tradition is unique in its suspicion that the demands of morality resist this kind of codification. But, for those of us who've been caught up in the attempt to codify the ethics of Jesus, the Confucian emphases on context-sensitivity and the centrality of the master-apprentice relationship for the cultivation of the moral life may call attention in a new way to the emphasis on discipleship in Jesus' strategy for bringing his students into his Way.

Back to Enemy Love

Nick and Ryan are both serious about making progress toward the kind of enemy love on display in the life and teachings of Jesus. And they've both been working hard at it for about four years. But they've adopted very different strategies for making progress.

Nick's strategy has been to study the Bible carefully in order to discern those principles and rules taught in scripture and that bear on response to injury and opposition. He's spent the past four years pouring over the teachings of the New Testament. He learned the languages in which the original autographs were written in order to better ascertain any nuances that might be lost in translation. He's considered carefully all of the better-known interpretations of the relevant passages. While he's too humble to suggest that he can now articulate definitively the Way of Jesus with respect to enemy love, he takes himself to have made significant progress toward that end. Nick can tell you in some detail what the principles are that govern a biblical response to injury and opposition. Given complex moral hypotheticals, he can deftly apply these principles and articulate the response mandated by the ethics of Jesus. And folks recognize as much. They often come to him when they're curious about the biblical principles that bear on this or that circumstance. And he's not forgotten the goal of all of this. He himself is doing his level best to live in accordance with the principles he's extracted from the teachings of Jesus.

Ryan's strategy has been very different. He's found someone widely recognized as embodying the Way of Jesus in the context of injury and opposition; someone willing to take him on as an apprentice. And Ryan's been pouring all of his energy into the imitation of this master. For every hour that Nick has spent studying New Testament Greek, Ryan has spent an hour in careful observation and imitation of his master. He has shadowed his master at work. And he pays special attention to him in the context of adversity. He's noticed, for example, that his master always clasps his hands together behind his back when responding to an aggressor in conversation. He's talked to his master about that and has learned that he uses this posture as a subtle reminder to himself that self-defense is not the priority in conversation. He's noticed that his master refuses to interrupt; often allowing an aggressive conversant to rant at length. He patiently waits his turn in the conversation with the result that he sometimes doesn't get a turn at all. He's noticed that his master, even when given the opportunity to respond, will sometimes surrender the last word in the conversation to the other. On the other hand, he's noticed that his master will sometimes quite forcibly interject with a point in conversation. In conversation, he's learned that his master is trying to eradicate his own personal need for getting the last word or for making points in conversation. At the same time, he sometimes recognizes that love for the other requires that a particular point be made.

Ryan takes on these and others of his master's practices whether or not he sees the relevance of those practices to his desired end (progress toward enemy love). He simply follows. He does with his time and energy what his master does with time and energy. And in time, he's found that the practices, responses, patterns of speech, thought and feeling — even facial expressions — which once came through considerable effort at imitation are increasingly his own. They come naturally. If asked to articulate the principles that govern his action, he'd be at something of a loss. He might just point to the master and say "I'm trying to do it like him." When given complex moral hypotheticals and asked what he would do, he's often uncertain. And while he's too humble to think of himself as having approximated the way of his master, folks around him have noticed the increasingly strong resemblances.

Suppose we know nothing other than what has been said here about Nick and Ryan. Whom should we be more confident is making serious progress toward a life of genuine enemy love? For Confucius, the answer is easy; we should be more confident that Ryan is making progress. Nick may or may not be making progress. We're not told enough to know. Having extracted a collection of principles from the scriptures is no guarantee that one will actually love one's enemies (even if one tries very hard to live in accordance with the principles so extracted). There is little if any correlation in Christian circles between expertise in the scriptures and actual ability to love one's enemies.

Reflection on the Confucian Way can alert us to the degree to which we've overestimated the efficacy of codified ethics for making actual moral progress.

I get mixed responses in conversations about Nick and Ryan. Some find that they're more confident about Ryan. But when asked to reflect on their own strategies heretofore, they find that they've approached things more like Nick. For such a person, reflection on the Confucian Way can bring to light a tension between their beliefs about how best to make moral progress on the one hand and their existing strategies for making moral progress on the other.

So what should Dantes have done?

I'm not sure. This much seems clear: Jesus would have him to love his enemies. He would have him promote, as much as it is in his power to do, their flourishing. Would that have meant treating them in just the way that he would have treated his friends? I doubt it. That would not have been good for him. And it would not have been good for them. Quite likely, the loving response to his oppressors would include (at least for a time, and maybe a long time) extreme caution, self-protection, and guarded distance.

And our felt desire to have justice rain down on Dantes' oppressors at his own bidding, while perhaps polluted by desires for vengeance and the like, is not from nowhere. It can often be very much for the good of the oppressor to be confronted by the oppressed if and when they are ready to do so. There is redemptive power both for the perpetrator and the victim of evil in loving confrontation. Dantes' loving response to his oppressors, whatever shape it should take, should be sensitive to and conditioned by the fact that they are his oppressors, not his friends.

And, given the virtually infinite array of variables governing appropriate response in any particular circumstance, it's not likely that the same response will be appropriate for each of his oppressors. For each, there will be a very particular history and often very subtle relational dynamics to which the good person would have to be sensitive. While good novelists give us a glimpse into the relational dynamics involved in particular interpersonal relationships they depict, it would be a novel of unreadable length that gave us everything we needed to know to proscribe any very particular path of action for Dantes.

It is, in part, for this reason that The Way of Confucius is ineffable. It can be recognized, learned, and known. One can move more and more fully into it. But it cannot be adequately *described*. It's far too complex. The good person knows the Way tacitly — knows it in a way that resists complete and sufficient description.

So far, then, I've argued that attention to the Confucian Way might help us out of the attempt to extract a collection of moral principles or rules for governing behavior in any and all circumstances from the teachings of Jesus. It frees us, for example, from the attempt to extract abstract principles from which can be deduced the proper response to a particular enemy. And it frees us from the attempt to extract abstract principles from which can be deduced a position on which car Ethan should drive or whether or not he should continue his tithe or grow succulents.

But doesn't this leave us without any particular guidance? For the morally serious among us, it will be unsatisfying in the extreme to be left with moral platitudes like "do your best to promote the flourishing of everyone." "Very well" one might say, "but how do I do *that?*" What should one do to affect the flourishing of those with whom one has contact? Is it not appropriate to expect more concrete behavior guidance from Jesus or from the great moral guides of human history?

Yes. In chapter five we will consider the Confucian category of *li* or "ritual" in connection with the undeniable need for concrete guidance in order to make discernable progress toward moral goodness. For the Confucian (and, I'll argue, for Jesus), the moral life is *both* characterized by spontaneity and facilitated by strict adherence to ritual.

For now, though, the lesson has been that there is no perfectly general principle to be articulated, memorized, and mastered, adherence to which will guarantee that one is living a good life in the presence of one's enemy. Nor is there a principle to be articulated, memorized, and mastered, adherence to which will guarantee that one's stewardship of one's resources is biblical. The postures, behaviors, and attitudes of the good person in response to oppression (and everything else) will be conditioned not only by the dispositions of her own heart but also by skilled discernment of the often subtle relational dynamics at work in any particular circumstance. This may be frustrating. It's hard to shake the desire for a clean (and, dare we hope, simple) articulation of the demands of morality for all circumstances.

But shake that desire we must. And an interaction with the Confucian approach to morality can be of some assistance in the effort. Morality is more complicated than is commonly supposed (and it's commonly supposed to be quite complicated as it is). Not only must we have a clear view of the ideals and principles at work in the moral dimension, we must also know ourselves. And we must know how we are situated within the relational dynamics of our circumstances if we're to respond with wisdom, love, and goodness.

CHAPTER 5

RITUAL

*At thirty, I stood firm. At forty, I had no doubts. At fifty, I knew
the decrees of Heaven. At sixty, my ear was an obedient organ
for the reception of truth. At seventy, I could follow what my
heart desired, without transgressing what was right.*

ANALECTS 2.4

*Every good tree bears good fruit, but a bad tree bears bad fruit.
A good tree cannot bear bad fruit, and a bad tree cannot bear
good fruit.*

MATTHEW 7:17-18

"I HAVE TRIED TO live my life without breaking a single rule."
Who can forget these lines delivered at the end of what can
only be described as a life of impressive moral seriousness? Victor
Hugo's infamous inspector, not unlike the incarnate God as he is
sometimes depicted on the cross, would sooner see his own demise
than suffer an unchecked infraction of the rules that govern human
behavior and interaction. For all of his moral seriousness, though, we
detect something deeply wrong with Javert's pursuit of justice. It is
maximally rigid, unnatural, and lacking spontaneity. Javert is a moral
sphex; unable to make the adjustments to his moral understanding

demanded by the complex conditions in which he finds himself. His morality is insensitive to the very human condition it seeks to honor and, for that reason, we find it deeply de-humanizing. Javert's rules, like John Irving's cider-house rules, seem imposed from a perspective that fails to anticipate present realities. They don't make sense in the context to which they're being so strictly applied. And to follow them is to depart dramatically from what would surely be the natural and spontaneous response of the person worthy of imitation.

Jean Valjean's moral seriousness takes an entirely different form. It is spontaneous and uncalculated. It seems to flow naturally from a basic orientation of grace and love — an orientation born not of having mastered a code of conduct, but of having been himself on the receiving end of mercy and forgiveness. His behavior comes to us not as the deliverance of a calculated ethic but rather of the free and natural expression of his heart. He is, as a consequence, a little bit unpredictable. And we love him.

We love him because we love spontaneity. We love it in kids. We love it in music, art, and literature. The trained musician can hear the difference between a technically flawless performance and a technically flawless performance that exhibits the natural and easy flow of spontaneity. The latter is the expression of the artist's having internalized the spirit of the piece. The former is, by comparison, robotic; inhuman. The same is true of the good life. Our moral sensibilities alert us to the possibility of a life lived in perfect conformity with the highest ethical standards but that fails to be good — fails to be good by virtue of its failing to be an expression of the heart.

Of course we wish (in our better moments) to abide by the highest of ethical standards. But we want more than that. We want authenticity. We want the life we live to be the true expression of our deepest self. So here's the rub. Our moral sensibilities demand a certain degree of spontaneity; freedom to act from the heart — the gut. On the other hand, we recognize that life untethered from moral authorities beyond ourselves will trend toward disaster. Our hearts are twisted. We see ourselves in William Golding's stranded boys. Amidst life's shadows and tall trees our hearts stand ready to spontaneously respond out of fear, insecurity, selfishness, and hate.

The spontaneous disposition of the human heart is not (or is not often enough) anything like the natural grace and love so evident in Jean Valjean. As much as we love him, we know that his way is not (or not for us anyway) the natural way, the easy way. And, for most of us, this is true whether or not we have, ourselves, been on the receiving end of profound love, mercy, and forgiveness. If we're going to live a life of love and grace toward others, we'll need to depart from what comes naturally to us. We'll need to commit to behaviors, postures, and attitudes imposed upon us from the outside.

Must we choose, then, between these two things for which our heart longs? Can we have the spontaneous life — a life characterized by the natural, uncalculated expression of who we are — only at the cost of forgoing the morally attractive life — a life lived in conformity with what we all know to be good and right?

Confucius (and those who followed in his intellectual wake) thought not. In his intellectual setting, there were powerful schools of thought on either side of the choice we've been considering. On the one hand, the Taoists prized spontaneity. They eschewed anything that might hinder the full expression of the inner condition of the heart. The Way, they thought, is in all of us. Our problem has not to do with the condition of our heart but with the myriad impediments to its being known and expressed. The path to the good life, then, comprises the steady removal of constraints and the consequent free

expression of the inner person. The Taoists would not have appreciated *The Lord of the Flies.*

On the other hand, the Legalists were deeply suspicious of the
human heart. Our only hope for peaceable coexistence, they thought,
was to curb the selfish and hateful dispositions of the heart by means
of a strictly enforced rule of law. The legalists would have thought the
character Jean Valjean — someone for whom the natural expression
of the heart is selfless love and grace — an utterly unrealistic ideal.

The Confucian tradition refuses to choose. It insists both on the
ideal of spontaneity *and* on the need for training — the need for
instruction from *without.* Confucius could appreciate the spontaneous goodness of Jean Valjean as an attainable good. At the same
time, he recognized that our hearts require training and redirection
if we're to find The Way. Jesus too, it seems, appreciated both the
need for law and the ideal of spontaneous goodness. He brilliantly
anticipated a misunderstanding of his message that would have ren-
dered the Old Testament law irrelevant and insisted on its continued importance for the pursuit of God. At the same time, among
his favorite metaphors for life in his Way was the fruit-producing
tree. Just as peaches naturally proceed from the inner nature of the
peach tree, goodness simply proceeds from the inner nature of the
good person. There is a kind of naturalness and spontaneity that
animates the good life as Jesus envisioned it. The goal, it seems, is to
live a life in conformity with the law that flows naturally and spontaneously from the heart, not from slavish, forced, and inflexible
adherence to its demands. It was part of the prophetic vision of the
good life under the reign of Messiah that the people would finally
have righteousness written *on their hearts,* presumably as opposed
to being written on a tablet or scroll somewhere to be memorized
and obeyed. There was from the beginning an anticipated return

to easy, natural, spontaneous righteousness under the direction of God's Messiah.

And this is precisely where the Confucian school of thought may be of some assistance. Whereas it has been characteristic of the Western philosophical tradition to emphasize choice and decision in the attempt to understand the good life, those following in the wake of Confucius were more interested in the cultivation of a well-styled life — one from which goodness was the spontaneous and natural fruit. Pursuit of ethical theory in the West occupied itself largely with the discovery and articulation of principles from which could be deduced the good choice — the right action — in any particular circumstance. On the other hand, and because of his insistence on *both* spontaneity and the need for training, ethical theory in the wake of Confucius occupied itself largely with the discovery of practices that would shape a person in such a way that goodness would be their natural disposition. The practices themselves (referred to as rituals or *li*) are imposed from the outside. To the untutored, they will likely feel unnatural. And The Way is characterized by strict adherence to them. The effect of this strict and unnatural adherence, though, is the cultivation of a life styled in such a way as to bring forth natural, easy, and contagious goodness.

In his book, *Learning from Asian Philosophy,* Joel Kupperman explains that the Confucian tradition, in its attempt to articulate a path to *natural* goodness, can alert us to the ambiguity of the word "natural." We are better positioned to make sense of a life governed by strict adherence to ritual *and* in pursuit of natural and spontaneous goodness once we see that there are several senses in which a behavior, posture, or attitude can be natural.

In one sense, something can be natural in that it is an expression of, or in good keeping with, the nature of the thing in question.

Absent impediments or dysfunction, there are ways of being in the world dictated by the inner structure of a thing. It is in the nature of the human person to develop a body with certain characteristics, to breath, to blink. It is natural for humans to walk upright and for dogs to walk on all fours. It would be the unnatural tomato plant that produced both tomatoes and snow peas. And it would be the unnatural fish that craved life on dry land. So we sometimes talk of something's being natural in our attempt to articulate how a thing will respond to its environment simply in virtue of the kind of thing that it is.

Other times, though, we say that something is natural and we mean that its occurrence requires no special or strenuous effort. We say in connection with Susan's tennis ability that "she's a natural." Here we're not talking about the *kind* of thing Susan is. Arguably she is the same *kind* of thing as is Sarah and Sarah is terrible at tennis. Rather, we are saying that the skill with which Susan plays tennis came to her much more easily than did similar skills in others. There may be others who play tennis with more skill than does Susan. When we call Susan "a natural" we're not commenting on her skill level *per se.* We're commenting on the particular way in which that skill has come to her. We're saying that it came with very little effort. It was somehow wired in from the beginning. In a similar vein, we may say of hospitality, generosity, envy, and myriad other traits both positive and negative that some folks come by them *naturally.* They (unlike other beings of the same kind) are somehow predisposed to their manifestation. So we sometimes talk of something's being natural when we mean to refer to the relative absence of effort or training involved in that thing's being manifest.

Were these to exhaust the possibilities for something's being natural, it would be very difficult to make sense of the suggestion that the good life is *both* the natural expression of the inner life of the moral hero *and* the result of arduous effort and training. After all, no amount of training can alter the *kind* of thing you are. So the concept of training seems utterly out of place with respect to the first conception of naturalness. On the other hand, you certainly *can* work and train to be more hospitable or better at tennis. But the degree of effort or training required for you will be inversely correlated with the degree to which we would count those things "natural" for you in the second sense. In this second sense, something is natural for you *just in so far* as it does *not* come as a consequence of effort or training. If we're to understand the proper relationship between effort and natural, spontaneous goodness, we need a third concept of the natural.

For the Confucian, there is a third sense in which something can be natural. And it is this third sense that is crucial for understanding the prospects and strategy for progress toward the good life. This third kind of naturalness is that of *trained spontaneity.* There are things that come naturally for us but only as a consequence of regiment of training that has been natural in *neither* of the previously considered senses. The regiment of training is not an expression of the kind of thing we are — it is not something that comes to us just by virtue of being a human person. But neither is it an expression of those dispositions with which we simply find ourselves in the world. It is a regiment that comes to us entirely from the outside and that demands strict adherence if we're to make progress toward the spontaneity we seek.

I made the mistake of teaching myself to play guitar during my freshman year in college. My roommate came back to the dorm from his first *real* guitar lesson and taught me the opening riff from Jon Bon Jovi's *I'm a Cowboy.* I was hooked. I bought my first guitar and learned to read chord charts. Before long, my playing (to my ear, anyway) was practically indistinguishable from that of Jon Bon Jovi himself.

Several months into my guitar "education," though, I discovered the need for bar chords and my inability to play them. I was unable to play them because I had never been taught how properly to position my left hand on the neck of the guitar. What came natural to me was to rest my entire thumb against the back of the neck while positioning the other four fingers in accordance with the chord charts I'd learned to read. And that position, it turns out, makes it extremely difficult to "reach" many of the bar chords I was hoping to play — makes them feel uncomfortable; unnatural; forced. What was required, as anyone who has taken *real* guitar lessons can tell you, was to rest only the tip of my thumb against the neck of the guitar. This gives you more reach and flexibility for the things you'll want to do if you progress in your guitar playing.

But playing with only the tip of my thumb on the neck of the guitar felt unnatural, forced. I had to force myself to position my hand that way *even when I didn't need to* in order for the more complicated chords to come naturally to me later on. In time, the bar chords came more naturally. They required less thought, less intention, less effort. The seemingly unnatural placement of my thumb on the neck of the guitar, over time, became natural. And it enabled natural and spontaneous abilities that would otherwise have been out of reach for me.

Mastery of almost every life skill requires this kind of trained spontaneity. In my martial arts class, we spent hours upon hours repeating "basic motions." Low block. High block. Front kick. Side kick. Every movement was scrutinized. A very slightly-over-rotated hip is brought into alignment by a skilled instructor. A stance that is an inch or two narrow is gently (or not so gently) nudged apart. The movements feel unnatural at first. But repetition builds muscle memory. Finally, you're given the opportunity to spar. And the movements that, at the beginning of training, were forced, intentional, and unnatural, become the instinctive and natural responses to the moves and countermoves of your sparring partner. These movements are not natural expressions of my nature as a human being. Nor am I somehow naturally gifted with the untrained and natural disposition to move in the ways dictated by the acquired art (one learns quickly to hate those in one's martial arts class who are so gifted). But, with training, the basic motions became natural to me. They became the uncalculated, unplanned, natural, and spontaneous response to the moves of my sparring partner.

But here's the really interesting thing. Watching a master martial artist in the context of sparring, you almost never see a "perfectly executed" motion. No perfectly executed high blocks. No perfectly executed side kicks. None of the motions are performed as they are when the master is training (and instructing others) in the basic motions. Rather, they are *perfectly adapted* to the particular movements and counter-movements of the sparring partner. They're unrepeatable because no sparring session is exactly like any other. A forearm held at too sharp an angle may be just the thing given the angle of attack from the sparring partner, but that angle would have been immediately corrected in repetitive training for the high block. The training is precise, predictable, exacting, calculated, and intentional. The consequence is the capacity to respond naturally and spontaneously to the imprecise and unpredictable circumstances of the sparring context. The master responds instinctively with a high block. But it is not the high block of repetitive training in basic motions. It is the unpredictable and unrepeatable motion that is a precise fit for this particular circumstance. And it comes instinctively to the master precisely because of his repetitive practice of a motion that, strictly speaking, would have been ineffective at this particular moment.

Students of the martial arts are continually tempted by two errors. The first is to resist the exacting correction of the master during training in basic motions. Having tasted the chaos of sparring, they're tempted to think that such precision has no real-life application. What's the point, they think, of a perfectly positioned forearm during training in basic motions if a perfectly-positioned forearm will virtually never be the appropriate response to my sparring partner? They fail to appreciate the (admittedly somewhat mysterious) bearing of precision in training to the appropriateness of response in sparring.

The second mistake is the more subtle of the two. It is the failure to make the jump from precision in training with basic motions to the trained but natural and spontaneous response to the sparring partner. The student is stiff in competition. His response to a punch may be a perfectly-executed high block. But it's an ineffectual block because this particular attack called for something with a slightly off-angled forearm. A good instructor will detect stiffness of this sort and will adjust the training in such a way as to encourage spontaneity, fluidity, and freedom to depart from the motions exacted upon the student during training in basic motions.

Training for excellence in almost any human endeavor (including guitar-playing and martial arts) involves this complicated interplay between precision in training and spontaneity "when it counts." We train with precision under the tutelage of a master. We do *exactly* what is proscribed by the master — even when we're not exactly sure why. We do not deviate from the master's instruction to accommodate our current natural inclinations. We do it like the master even when it's unnatural, forced, intentional, calculated. The training may feel inauthentic and irrelevant. But we trust the master. And we realize that it may be a long time before the training has as its effect that we can respond both spontaneously and appropriately. Meanwhile, we trust the training. Confucius seems to have thought that his heart could not be trusted to respond spontaneously and appropriately until the age of seventy!

Reflection on the Confucian tradition can sensitize us to the possibility of a *trained* kind of spontaneity.

Christians, it seems, are tempted by exactly these two errors. On the one hand, we're tempted to resist precise, repetitive ritual. It can feel inauthentic, unnatural, calculated, intentional, forced. It often has no obvious applicability to real life beyond the ritual. For that reason, and because of the sheer repetitiveness of the training, it can feel like "just going through the motions." We fail to appreciate the bearing that ritual has on the ability to respond *both* spontaneously *and* appropriately to the chaos of life. We embrace the beauty of spontaneity and natural goodness without proper appreciation for the fact that it is a *trained* spontaneity enjoined on us by the teachings of Jesus.

For Christians who've been trained into a subtle suspicion of ritual, reflection on the Confucian emphasis on *trained spontaneity* may create a category for understanding its importance. We sing the same prayers (and in the same key). We celebrate the same holidays with the same activities. We say the same things before and after we read the scriptures. We pass the peace of Christ to one another and with the same words. Over and over and over again. We do it with precision. And we correct the smallest of departures from the way it has always been done — the way it has been done by the masters. We are not free to observe Lent in just any way we like, for example. We observe it in a way passed down to us over the millennia by masters in the Way of Jesus. We do it the way they've done it. Along the way, we are very slowly shaped and molded into a style of life that would never have emerged from the inner dispositions of our hearts and that we could never have invented for ourselves. And we acquire humble appreciation for — indeed, a felt dependence upon — those who've gone before us. We find some freedom from the grip of Western individualism and its invitation to create our own rituals and practices — rituals and practices chosen for their capacity to satisfy our own personal tastes and preferences.

On the other hand, we sometimes fail to make the jump from the calculated, precise, and highly intentional character of practice and ritual to the spontaneous fluidity of loving response to God and neighbor. We bring the beautifully scripted words and practices of the Christian dojo into the shadows and tall trees of life and wonder at their ineffectiveness. We take offense when the behavior, the words, the responses of our fellow Christians fail to conform to the principles and the script so often rehearsed in church and in the other centers of Christian education. We're tempted to accuse those Christians who depart from the script of living a kind of double life. They would *never* talk like that or act like that in church, we think. And we fail to see that this response to neighbor, while it fails to be a perfect "basic motion" is in fact a *perfectly adapted* motion for the particular circumstance in question. It isn't (and shouldn't be) *practiced* in just that way. It could not have been predicted. And it's unlikely to be repeated. But such is the character of the great sparring match of life. We practice, not in order to perform the precise practiced motions when it counts, but in order to stand ready to respond appropriately, spontaneously, and naturally.

For Christians with too rigid a conception of the Way of Jesus as it gets expressed in the chaotic circumstances of life, then, reflection on the Confucian emphasis on *trained spontaneity* may bring with it a new freedom to enjoy the *spontaneous* side of the good life for which our hearts and our moral sensibilities call out. Over time we're afforded the opportunity to relax and lean into our training. Sparring is so much more enjoyable when you learn to relax into it — to stop thinking about and trying to perform the basic motions. You simply respond to your partner and you learn to trust that the precision of your training will have as its effect the spontaneous and appropriate response in the moment. Life, for the Confucian master, is a kind of dance. The moves are choreographed, practiced, regimented. But, when it counts, they're also spontaneous and natural. They never happen in exactly the same way twice. Having been shaped by the regiment of a rule of life, the good person finds that good fruit is simply the natural product of the person they've become.

The Confucian ideal of *trained spontaneity,* then, opens up the possibility of a life that is *both* informed by a Way that is not our own *and* spontaneous, natural, and free. Just as martial arts training involves a complicated back-and-forth between the precision of training in basic motions and the chaotic spontaneity of sparring, the Christian life can involve a complicated back-and-forth between the precision of training in the practices of Jesus and the great ones of the faith and the chaotic spontaneity of neighbor and enemy love in "real life." We are *both* free, uncalculated, unthinking, *and* deeply shaped by strict adherence to a standard and a Way that comes to us from the outside. We are shaped by regiment, ritual, and practice. And as a consequence, we are increasingly capable of acting from the desires and natural dispositions of the heart.

Finally, reflection on the Confucian emphasis on trained spontaneity can liberate us from the preoccupation, so characteristic of Western thought about ethics and morality, with big ethical moments. For those of us who take the moral life seriously, it's easy to allow our attention to be dominated by reflection on moral choices that have dramatic consequences for our lives or the lives of those we love. We fixate on "moral dilemmas" and try to discern rational principles for their resolution. Would it be ok to cause the death of one person to save four? Should I cheat on my taxes if the money saved will be used to alleviate the suffering of the impoverished? Should I accept my brother's invitation to stand witness to his same-sex marriage despite my conviction that same-sex marriage is unbiblical?

And it's understandable that these moments should capture our attention. These are, after all, the moments when the structure of our deepest convictions is laid bare. We, all of us, are for the alleviation of the suffering of the impoverished, for example. But how does this value stack up against our deeply held conviction that we shouldn't cheat on our taxes? So we look to reason or revelation for a principled reason to prioritize some of our values over the others in order to discern the strongest ethical position vis-à-vis these and countless other dilemmas.

But the truth is that we're really very infrequently faced with genuine moral dilemmas. Most of our lives are lived in the mundane crystal clarity of right and wrong. Most who cheat on their taxes are not doing so in order to facilitate famine relief. They're doing it so they can keep their new boat. And when the moments of genuine dilemma arise (and they certainly do arise), psychologists will tell us that we're far more conditioned to a particular resolution of the dilemma than we appear to ourselves to be — even as we coolly consider options before us. Our character, style, habits, and dispositions make it far more predictable than we'd like to think in which direction we'll go.

The Confucian tradition, with its emphasis on trained spontaneity, encourages reflection on the practices conducive to the character, habits, and dispositions favorable to doing the right thing *in advance of* the moments of big decision and dilemma. The emphasis is on practicing a way of life in imitation of the Master in the mundane day-to-day of moral clarity. The big ethical moment — the dilemma — is precisely the time to relax into one's character and act from the heart. It's the moment when, increasingly and as appropriate training takes hold, one can simply do what one knows in one's gut is the right thing to do.

Jesus, undoubtedly, had many big ethical moments. Among the most significant was his confrontation with the Roman guards who affected his gruesome death on the cross. A teacher of mine used to ask (rhetorically, I think) whether it was easy or hard for Jesus to bless those Roman guards — to request forgiveness on their behalf from his father. No doubt it was hard. Everything is hard, I suppose, when you're suffering in the way he suffered. But would it have been easier or harder for him to curse his oppressors? Which came more naturally, more spontaneously, out of the heart of the Messiah? A curse for those at whose hands he was to suffer and die? Or a self-forgetful blessing and an expression of deep desire for the flourishing of these, his enemies? And who is the more impressive moral hero? The one who is somehow able to force a blessing against every urge to curse his oppressors? Or a person for whom love of enemy is so deeply rooted that a blessing is the spontaneous, uncalculated, and natural response?

Arguably, Jesus was the sort of man for whom the curse would have felt like going aggressively against the grain. His response was born not out of the ability to give careful thought to the structure of his moral principles, but out of a heart conditioned by long-honored practices that conformed his heart to the heart of his father. It was, I should think, what he did in the monotonous moral clarity of the day-to-day that conditioned him to spontaneously love his enemies in the way he did on the cross.

So how might a Confucian think about Inspector Javert and Jean Valjean? Clearly the morality of Javert, while impressive in its serious-ness, is far too inflexible and forced to be attractive to the Confucian sensibility. But what about Valjean? Is this a compelling portrait of the moral hero? I don't think so. Valjean exhibits the spontaneous and natural goodness so central to the Confucian picture of the good life. But his, so far as we can tell, is not a *trained* spontaneity. He has a life-transforming experience of grace and forgiveness when Bishop Bienvenu "gives him back to God." And that seems to have been sufficient to turn him from a life of self-preservation, pride, and contempt for authority to a person from whom flowed naturally acts of grace and forgiveness even to those in authority from whom he experienced oppression. What is missing is any indication that the spontaneous goodness that issued from the heart of Valjean came as a consequence of anything like *training*.

Perhaps there are genuine Jean Valjeans in the world — people whose basic orientation and posture are utterly transformed by a single experience of grace and forgiveness. But the Confucian would quickly remind us that this is not the norm. For most of us, unexpected experiences of radical grace and forgiveness *mark* us. And they may change us in various ways. But they rarely *reorient* us in the way that Valjean's life was reoriented. Such reorientation requires the slow business of training and imitation in the Way of a master. Jesus recognized this. No doubt that's why he took as long as he did in the discipleship of his students. In very short order, he could have offered each a profound experience of love, grace, forgiveness, and acceptance. This could have been followed by the handing over of a pristine theology — those teachings needful for the pursuit of life in the Kingdom. Instead, he was careful to postpone his crucifixion long enough to give them the opportunity for sustained imitation.

The invitation stands today. Would-be followers of Jesus today have not only the teachings of the Master but the added advantage of deep reflection on the Way he recommends by skilled practitioners of His Way throughout the ages. The Confucian would not expect immediate reorientation to be the natural consequence of the sympathetic reception of these teachings. Rather, to approach these teachings with expectations natural to the Confucian is to mine them for recommended practices in the mundane moral clarity of the day-to-day that will have as their fruit the spontaneous goodness of the Master in the big ethical moments.

CHAPTER 6

SAM

WHAT MIGHT IT look like to pursue a life of discipleship to Jesus that incorporates wisdom from the Confucian tradition? It might look a million different ways, of course. If there is one thing upon which Confucius would insist, it's that The Way will vary depending on the context of practice. Sometimes, though, it's easier to envision a path for yourself having been acquainted with the concrete path of another. This is why novels, stories, movies, and other narrative forms of expression are essential for moral education. They're not the best tools for the concise presentation of particular ideas, and they usually fail as compelling narratives when they attempt as much. But they stir the imagination. And in so doing, they sometimes open up vistas from which to envision for ourselves paths and strategies that might not present themselves as readily as when we consider ideas presented in more didactic terms. In the preceding chapters, we've been primarily concerned with the articulation of general themes and emphases that find powerful expression in the Confucian tradition. This chapter attempts a kind of snap-shot of a particular life in pursuit of Confucian Christian ideals.

Six years ago, Sam attended a series of apologetics seminars at his church. In the first session, students were introduced to the notion of a "world view" and to the central tenets of "the Christian worldview." Sam still remembers his initial puzzlement at the use of the definite article in that expression. Was there just one way to view the world as a Christian? Each subsequent session took aim at some worldview other than the Christian worldview. The central tenets of the worldview in question were explained with particular attention given to those dimensions of the worldview at odds with the Christian worldview. Reasons were given for rejecting alternative worldviews in favor of the Christian worldview.

For Sam, the class backfired when it came to its treatment of Confucianism. Students were presented with just a few short sections of the Confucian *Analects,* which Sam found to be brilliantly provocative. He found himself mulling them over at night. And when he quoted them with friends, they proved themselves to be fertile soil for deep and interesting conversation.

But Confucianism was presented as a "this-worldly" worldview — one that placed near exclusive emphasis on goodness and flourishing in "this world." It was never made entirely clear in the class what it meant to call a world "this world." What world could there possibly be beyond "this one," he wondered. To be sure, Sam believed in dimensions of this world that received little or no attention in Confucianism as it was presented in his class. But he also thought it incumbent upon Christians to promote flourishing in those dimensions of this world explicitly addressed by the Confucian masters. So he wondered at the suggestion that the Confucian worldview should be rejected *tout court* for its "this-worldliness." We don't refuse to incorporate into our worldview the deliverances of chemistry just because chemistry leaves important dimensions of this world (say, the elements of good poetry) unexamined.

Beyond his this-worldliness, though, Confucius was presented as having opposed the biblical idea that we should treat our enemies in just the way that we treat our friends. Moreover, the *Analects*, it was suggested, would have us to reject anything like an absolute codified ethic that could be consulted to determine once for all whether or not an action type is morally permissible. The Confucian ethic, it was suggested, is radically circumstance-relative and therefore relativistic. These things bothered Sam. He knew that Jesus would have us to love our enemies and he was reluctant to give up on absolute truth when it comes to right and wrong. On the other hand, he wondered whether the Christian injunction to love your enemies really meant that you had to treat them just like your friends. And the Confucian *Analects* certainly didn't *read* like an endorsement of relativism. Confucius, it seemed, had very particular ideas about how to find your way into flourishing. He certainly didn't *seem* to be telling his students to do whatever they thought was right. Quite the opposite in fact.

Confucius was also presented as having no category for the biblical notions of sin and the fall. He taught, it was suggested, that human nature is "good" — that by simply following our natural inclinations we can find our way into flourishing. And the Confucian insistence on filial piety, it was suggested, was directly at odds with the call of Jesus to replace family loyalty with loyalty to communities of discipleship to himself. But to Sam, Confucius didn't *seem* to be telling his students to follow their natural inclinations. In fact, he said of himself that he couldn't follow his natural inclinations until his character had been shaped by seventy years of training in The Way. And Sam had a sneaking suspicion that it would be a *good* thing for communities of Jesus following if we learned to be better fathers, mothers, sons, daughters, spouses, and siblings.

So, quite despite the intentions of the teacher, the class sparked in Sam a desire to learn more from the Confucian *Analects* and from the Confucian tradition more generally. Beginning with the *Analects*, he started to read the masters in the Confucian tradition. He read them not in order to determine whether or not to *replace* his Christian commitment with a commitment to Confucianism. He read them in search of wisdom that would aid in his pursuit of the Way of Jesus. He's been reading and thinking about the Confucian way now for six years — long enough to see for himself some of its effect on his life. He thinks and feels differently about things than he did six years ago. And his approach to the Way of Jesus is slowly transforming into a Way recognizably informed by the themes and emphases that he has most appreciated in the Confucian literature.

Years before this class, Sam met his wife Gloria as a junior at UCLA. They dated for two years in college and were married shortly after graduation. He quickly landed a good job in an advertising firm. She finished with a degree in secondary education and began her credential program the following Fall. They found a small but pleasant apartment and began their life together. Both came from families that had settled for multiple generations in the Los Angeles area. So holidays were exhausting, especially after their daughter Gracie was born. The weeks leading up to every holiday were filled with negotiations and arguments about where to celebrate.

"Christmas with my family and New Years with yours?"

"But we did Christmas with your family last year. And New Years is no big deal for my family."

"Ok. How about Christmas Eve with your family and Christmas morning with mine?"

"But my family always celebrates on Christmas morning. How am I going to convince my brother and his family (not to mention my parents, and all of my aunts, uncles, and cousins) to change up our tradition?"

It was tiring. And, as it turned out, filling. Typically, they'd pack the mini-van, which was not a trivial task since the necessities included diaper bags, slings (yes . . . plural), a swinging nap chair, the pack-n-play and myriad other contraptions essential for Gracie's happiness and well-being. Then they would head to Sam's family celebration for the first part of the holiday (complete with a holiday feast). At mid-day, they'd re-pack the mini-van and head to Gloria's family celebration for the second part of the day (complete with holiday feast). Every holiday ended with Gracie in bed two hours after bedtime and an exhausted and overstuffed Sam and Gloria collapsed on the couch barely capable of speech.

And it wasn't just holidays. It was a complicated business trying to navigate the expectations of two relatively involved and local families of origin. Almost every decision of any significance — decisions about which church to attend, where and how the kids should be schooled, where to shop for their first home — surfaced disagreements (sometimes passionate disagreements) from these two families that had collided in the marriage of Sam and Gloria.

So when the offer came from Colorado Springs after three years living in their Los Angeles apartment, Sam saw it as their ticket to independence. Little Sammy was three months old. Gracie hadn't yet started school. It would be an easy transition for the kids. It was a far more lucrative position than had been his position in Los Angeles. So Gloria would have the option of staying home with the kids. And the move would facilitate the kind of independence that Sam had always thought would come more-or-less automatically when they got married. But it had not come automatically. They were still struggling to balance the task of starting a new family with the felt-responsibilities of being son, daughter, nephew, niece, brother, and sister in close proximity to families of origin.

Gloria's emotions were more of a mixture. Though exhausting, she experienced proximity to family as a deeply grounding part of the life they were creating together in Los Angeles. Her credentials would not transfer to Colorado. So the "option" of staying home with the kids felt more like *fait accompli*. And she wondered whether she'd find full-time child rearing as fulfilling and satisfying as had been her first two years of teaching. Still, she was excited about the vocational opportunity for Sam. And she too had a nagging suspicion that they'd not yet affected the "breaking away" that she'd been taught to think was essential to a healthy marriage.

So move they did. Some members of the family (on both sides) took it better than others. But most continued to communicate love and support. They bought a big house with a pool in the backyard and they quickly joined a large church where they found their way into new friendships. Sam's new job, though lucrative, proved to be much more demanding than he'd initially thought it would be. He'd often leave for work before the kids were up for breakfast and return just in time for a quick tuck-in at night. And weekends, if not spent working, were often spent worrying about work.

Gloria, as it turned out, *loved* being a full-time mom. She jumped at every opportunity to involve herself in the lives of her kids. She was a soccer mom, a leader on the PTA, and a homework tutor. And she reveled in it all. But her joy was tainted somewhat by a nagging and intermittent sense that Sam was missing it — missing this precious window of opportunity to parent together these precious souls. The visits to Los Angeles to be with family were increasingly infrequent. Gloria spent considerable time in communication with her family. But Sam's connection to family had been reduced to the obligatory phone calls on Christmas morning, mother's day, father's day, and (when he remembered) birthdays.

So Sam's initial interaction with the Confucian emphasis on filial piety and on the mastering of family relationships as the root of goodness occasioned a deep and painful reconsideration of the trajectory of his life. In the blink of an eye, Sammy was in third grade. Gracie was just a couple of years away from middle school. It was excruciating to think of all that he'd missed in the pursuit of his career. His relationships, many of them anyway, were shallow and marked by significant tension. His superiors at the office praised the quality of his work but found him difficult to manage. Performance reviews painted the picture of a highly efficient advertising expert who struggled to work effectively on a team.

At church he was respected but not known. Having been raised in the church, he knew his Bible. He could articulate a biblical ethic and there were no obvious respects in which his life was a departure from that code. As an outspoken defender of biblical perspectives on just about everything, he often found his way into the center of whatever conflict was animating the congregation at present (worship style, building projects, pastoral hiring decisions, etc.).

He and Gloria still loved each other deeply. But their evening conversations (infrequent as they were) often revolved around the many relational tensions and conflicts that characterized and dominated Sam's life with others. It was hard to identify anyone in Sam's life with whom he was significantly connected and with whom he was not experiencing significant tension. Sam chalked all of this up to the pressures of success in a stressful job. He didn't know anyone beyond work, church, Gloria, and the kids. And it felt like all he could possibly do to attend well enough to those relationships. He certainly didn't have time to get to know his neighbors or to attend to the needs of his broader community. It hadn't occurred to him that his failure to achieve healthy relationships at work, church, and elsewhere — not to mention the narrowing of the scope of his interpersonal concern — might be related to his having abandoned the project of mastering the basic relationships that comprise family.

In any case, Sam's early interactions with Confucianism occasioned for him a deep unhappiness with the overall direction that his life had taken. He was not finding his way more and more deeply into human-heartedness. Instead, he had increasingly experienced life as a kind of rat race — a series of obstacles and challenges to be overcome without running afoul of his biblical ethic. Somehow, his life felt less human now than it had felt at the beginning of his married life with Gloria. His life was full beyond capacity even though he was somehow significantly involved with fewer people than ever.

That was six years ago. A lot has changed in the years since that first encounter with the Confucian "world-view" in the apologetics class at church. And much is still changing as Sam continues to take aboard and internalize the wisdom he's discovering in the Confucian tradition he's been exploring.

For one, Sam is appreciating more and more the importance of practice in the art of submission and training in the habits characteristic of the effective follower. As a Christian, Sam has always been committed — even if only at the level of abstract theological theorizing — to the idea that we are to submit ourselves to God. But he has a deep appreciation now for his family as a place within which to practice and grow in the art of submission. When he drifted out of relationship with his parents, his grandparents, and his uncles and aunts, he cut away the only relationships within which he felt any pressure to practice genuine submission — the bending of one's will to that of another. That, he now recognizes, is what made holidays so complicated and difficult. He and Gloria were trying to work out the identity of their own nuclear family in the context of submission to their families of origin. As long as he lived in proximity to family, he couldn't bring himself simply to disregard his elders. He felt the very human impulse somehow to bend to their wishes.

Finding a balance, though, between submission and growth into the unique expression of family that was his to enjoy with Gloria and the kids proved to be a messy and difficult project — a project he now thinks should not have been abandoned. He realized six years ago that, apart from the mutual submission that (in theory, anyway) characterized his marriage, he was not genuinely submitted to anyone. Though he would sometimes seek advice from others, his life was his own to do with what he liked. And, as attractive as that kind of independence might have sounded a decade ago, it now strikes him as a recipe for deep loneliness.

So Sam's taken some aggressive steps to re-introduce filial piety and the opportunity for genuine submission into his life. He began by pursuing relationship with Saul. Saul is seventy-two. He's been walking with Jesus his whole life and anyone who spends time with him speaks of him as a sort of conduit of the palpable presence of Christ and his Kingdom Way. About four years ago, he agreed to meet every other Tuesday morning with Sam for coffee and they've been meeting ever since. Saul is reluctant to exercise anything like authority in his conversations with Sam. But Sam continually insists on being the *learner* in his relationship with Saul and, so far as he's able, treats Saul's gentle and reluctant suggestions as opportunities for practice in unquestioning obedience. If Saul mentions a book that has shaped him, Sam reads it. If Saul mentions a practice that has been helpful in his formation, Sam finds a way to incorporate that practice himself — whether or not he understands its value. Saul is passionate about eating right and, even more so, getting enough rest. So Sam's been eating differently and enforcing upon himself a "bedtime."

Through his relationship with Saul, Sam's learned quite a bit about how to follow well. He knows better than ever how to observe and engage someone when the goal is to conform. He asks different questions now over coffee than he did four years ago; questions that draw out of Saul precious gems about the good life that even Saul wouldn't have thought on his own to share. And slowly, in small but perceptible ways, Sam is becoming more like Saul. He thinks more like Saul, prays more like Saul, and engages others in conversation more like Saul. He's even unconsciously taken on some of Saul's mannerisms.

Perhaps even more significantly, Sam has re-established meaningful connection with his family. It was September 17th, five years ago, that he called his dad. That date stands out because there is nothing at all special about it. It's not a holiday. It's nobody's birthday. So the last thing in the world that Sam's dad was expecting that day was a phone call from his middle son. Sam apologized for having failed in his filial obligations as a son. He didn't mention all of his father's missteps (and there were plenty of them that he could have mentioned) in the attempt to hold family together while Sam and Gloria were trying to figure out their life together. He simply humbled himself before his father, acknowledged that he had treated his family badly, and expressed his desire to be reconnected. It's not been an easy road back. He's had to hear from several in his family how painful it was for them to have him treat family as something to be escaped — to be treated as people with whom to endure a phone call during the holidays but who are otherwise to be disregarded.

It took all of the humility he could muster to take those first steps toward his family. But things since have been changing. Over the past several years, he's re-established significant connection to his parents, his siblings, his aunts, uncles, cousins, and grandparents. The healing has been slower in some quarters than in others. But his growing ability to assume the position of the humble, unknowing, and submissive learner is speeding the process remarkably.

Holidays are messy again. Sam and Gloria haul the kids out to Los Angeles for family visits whenever they can. And every visit is an occasion for difficult conversations about how to divide the time. But Sam has a growing appreciation for the struggle. He now receives it not as something to be escaped but as a part of what it means to grow into that balance of submission and independence characteristic of the adult filial son. And life is somehow richer as he grows in his ability to think of himself, not as an individual, but as *one* part of this larger organism that stretches backward and forward through the generations. Whereas they rarely entered his consciousness a decade ago, the various members of his family come to mind often now. And when they do, it's not at all uncommon for them to get a quick call out of the blue from Sam; a call perhaps just to say "I was just thinking of the old tether-ball set in grandpa's backyard as I set up the new one for our kids. Remember that?"

Just recently, at a family gathering, someone acted in such a way as to offend and disrespect several of his aunts, uncles, and cousins. And he was offended for them — offended on their behalf. Ten years ago he would have *noticed* the offense. And he would have *judged* the behavior to be rude. But he would not have *felt* the offense in his own person. It was as if he, himself, had been disrespected. He felt the desire to make reparations somehow for these dear ones who had been wronged. As a result, they felt from him something like genuine sympathy and connection. And it was a beautiful thing. A human thing. Something into which he would never have entered ten short years ago.

He can feel that his heart has expanded in such a way as to receive in his own person what comes to the various members of his family (for better or worse). He feels honored when his parents receive honor. He feels disrespected when his aunts and uncles are disrespected. It's as though he's been growing an increasing number of receptors to honor, dishonor, shame, and praise. Life is bigger. It's more complicated. But it's richer. Though it's not clear to either of them how to make it work, Sam and Gloria have had conversations recently about moving back to Los Angeles. Life in proximity to extended family is messy. But they long for deeper involvement with these folks who have increasingly come to feel like extensions of themselves — or, perhaps more accurately, like fellow parts of a larger relational whole.

Things are different at home too. If you had asked Sam about "the good life" ten years ago, he'd have said that the most important thing is to figure out what the Bible requires and prohibits and to live in such a way as not to flout any biblical principles. Beyond that, if you can secure for yourself a big house, a pool, and a chunk of money to set aside for your kids' college education without running afoul of any biblical principles, all the better. These days, he's more sensitive to questions about a well-styled life. He's learned the hard way that you can steer clear of any biblical prohibitions and fail to flourish as a person.

Sam has also taken to heart Saul's gentle reminders that the opportunity to live with and raise your kids will come and go in what will feel like the blink of an eye when viewed from your 70's. Several years ago, he stopped working on Saturdays and he made the simple decision not to leave for work until his kids had left for school in the morning. These were scary decisions. And they were not without financial ramifications. But they haven't fired him yet. And, while his productivity isn't what it used to be, his social capital has multiplied at work as he's found it more and more natural to interact with the folks at work as one human to another. He actually wonders and asks them about their conceptions of the well-styled human life and he finds himself in the most interesting of conversations. His heart has expanded, it seems, in such a way as to incorporate some degree of genuine concern for these, his coworkers, as human beings worthy of his interest.

And it's not just his coworkers. As strange as it may seem, it took a conscious intention on Sam's part several years ago to engage his immediate neighbors in an actual conversation. Since that time, he's walked with his neighbors through painful divorces, the loss of loved ones, and the joys of new birth — events about which he would have been scarcely conscious ten years ago. Last year, despite the down-tick in his compensation at work and together with several others in his neighborhood, he had the profound joy of supporting a family in his neighborhood through a 6-month season of joblessness. Last month, he worked with his kids on the weekends to replace his front lawn with 6 raised irrigated garden beds. They sent flyers to the neighborhood inviting folks to claim a few square feet to grow whatever they'd like. His heart is expanding, it seems, to incorporate not only a deeper identification with his family but a genuine and heartfelt concern for folks at work and in his community. The Confucian idea that the good life is the life appropriately connected with others, and that connectedness *begins* with family and expands, is an increasingly felt reality for Sam.

Unfortunately, Sam's relationships are not all hugs and kisses. He's got enemies — folks who seem bent on the diminishing of his flourishing. Some of them are family members with whom it's been more difficult to get over the hurt generated by years of mutual mistreatment, neglect, and misstep. For years, Sam oscillated between two positions. In some seasons, he would wrestle with guilty feelings for having adopted the self-protective postures that come so naturally in the presence of someone who seems bent on hurting you (or, at least, indifferent to your pain). He would avoid, neglect, and rebuff. And he'd feel guilty about it. Something in him knew that this was not the way of enemy love so frequently endorsed in the teachings of Jesus. In other seasons, he would suffer the abuse that comes from opening yourself up to such a person in just the way that you would open yourself up to a friend. He's discovered repeatedly that this is as bad for them as it is for him. When one person's habit of hurting another is indulged, neither is the better for it.

Things are different now. He no longer bounces back and forth between neglect (together with the accompanying guilt) and wide-open vulnerable pursuit of the other (together with the accompanying subjection to predictable mistreatment). On the one hand, there are elements of his posture that continue to be guarded and self-protective. But he no longer neglects, avoids, or rebuffs. He is actively in pursuit of opportunities to love these folks. If there is an occasion to honestly and publicly honor them, or to privately and sincerely encourage them, he seizes upon it. He has not opened himself to them as to a friend. But he promotes their well-being in whatever way is available to him. And he holds out as the desire of his heart that theirs would be a relationship that moves in the direction of friendship and mutual affection. He disciplines his mind with routine reminders that the category of "enemy" is a temporary one — that there will come a day, sooner or later, when mutual love reigns in this relationship.

Sam's as passionate about the scriptures as ever he's been. But he's reading the scriptures differently these days. Sam used to read the Bible with two questions in mind: (i) What should be *affirmed* in order not to run afoul of biblical theology and (ii) what must I *do* (and refrain from doing) in order not to run afoul of biblical principles governing the moral life? Now, he reads with greater sensitivity to the grand narrative articulated in this rich and complex multi-genre collection. He reads in order to gain a deeper understanding of story of God's redemptive program in human history. He reads in order to project that narrative forward — to discern the movements of God toward his people today. He reads not primarily for information mastery (though there is information mastery that occurs) but for the purpose of finding his way more and more deeply into this divine conspiracy to bring the human experiment back to its intended trajectory.

Not much has changed in the *content* of his theology. He still affirms the orthodox and biblical creeds that have defined the Christian church for millennia. In fact, those creeds have greater significance for him than ever before. He used to think of them as boundaries beyond which lie "the others" — those who aren't quite deserving of the label "Christian." They were, he thought, the last word on those questions that define the Christian faith. Since he had never in his adult life really been tempted to flirt with the boundaries of Christian commitment, he had rarely considered with much energy these historical affirmations. Their role, he thought, was to give clear definition to the inside and the outside. But when you spend your whole life in the middle — miles and miles from the boundaries — you have little occasion to think about border patrol.

Now, he considers them routinely and with enthusiastic interest. They've become for him an avenue by which to achieve connection with his brothers and sisters in the Way of Jesus over the past two millennia — not to mention his contemporaries around the globe. These historical and biblical affirmations have drawn him into the study of Church history. By way of these affirmations, he finds his way into the conversations (indeed, the arguments) from which they arose. He now thinks of them not as the last word but as a kind of first and foundational word. We affirm these things together. And we work out their interpretation and application for our scene in the grand narrative. He's open to the idea that these interpretations and applications will give rise to new affirmations — affirmations that could not possibly have been foreseen or predicted by our predecessors in the faith. Biblical theology, for Sam, has become less a matter of articulating the last word on the big questions addressed in the scriptures and more about faithful continuance of the conversation birthed in the teachings of Jesus and the apostles.

To be faithful to the conversation is to retain what has been handed down to us by those who have gone before. It is to agree that whatever is said next will be shaped and guided by what has already been said. You can't say just anything you like and continue to contribute to a conversation. Sometimes people inadvertently talk themselves right out of the conversation of which they were previously a part. That's always an awkward thing for the other conversation participants who wish to continue the conversation. Suppose, for example, that we were all talking about favorite vacation spots. Jim started talking about Maui. But he's been talking for fifteen minutes without a break and for the past three or four minutes he's been talking about his Labrador retriever. He's left the conversation. He's no longer building on what came before. Faithfulness in conversation requires ongoing mindful attention to what has already been said.

One way to facilitate faithfulness is to habitually repeat the deliverances of scripture and the creeds. We remind ourselves what has been said so far to keep ourselves in conversation with our brothers and sisters in the faith. But a mere repeating of what has been said in the past is no conversation. Conversation (of any kind) always builds on what has been said and projects something new into the future. So doctrine has become personal for Sam. Whereas doctrine used to comprise a body of information to be mastered, affirmed, and repeated, and which functioned to define the inside and outside of his faith, it is now an avenue through which his heart has expanded to embrace and engage his brothers and sisters around the globe and stretching back through the ages. It's not just that he *knows* about these others and what they thought. He feels himself connected to them in a way that's hard for him to describe to anyone who doesn't feel it. It's as though a project of galactic significance has been handed down to him and to those with whom he practices the Way of Jesus. And he wants to do justice to those who carried the torch before.

So Sam's life has changed significantly. He's re-established connection to his family of origin and is finding his way back into those basic relational dynamics associated with being a son, a sibling, a nephew, etc. And he's gained a new appreciation for the art of following and the discipline of submission. He's practicing submission with his friend Saul and exploring the dimensions of submission appropriate to the various relationships comprising his extended family. He's making real decisions — decisions with real consequences — that prioritize his opportunity to be a father and an involved spouse.

Decreased investment at work has had as a result the move to a smaller house — one with a community pool instead of a private pool in his backyard. And he's not positive that his new approach to work will be sustainable in his current position. Again, they've not fired him yet. But the future feels less certain than when he was giving himself more fully to his work. A small but growing part of him hopes for the termination of his current employment as that might give his family just the push they need to move back to Los Angeles. He still crosses his fingers behind his back when he hopes for that. He's not quite ready to embrace it as the desire of his heart. But the idea is gnawing away at him.

He's more enthusiastic than ever before about the scriptures and about the history of orthodox Christian affirmations. In fact, he's found a group of men and women in his church interested in studying the history of Christian theology together. Beyond that, his time with the folks at church is spent very differently than it was before. Service on committees governing over decisions about new church facilities have given way to strategy sessions aimed at creative thinking about Christian loving postures toward prisoners, sexual minorities, and folks without adequate housing — folks at the margins of "accepted" society. Participants in these meetings wonder together how to love well these precious souls who have all-too-frequently experienced nothing but contempt and condemnation from all but the most radical of Jesus followers. Service on the committee for discerning the biblical constraints on worship style has given way to a weekly meeting with Christians in his neighborhood aimed at creative strategies for loving well those with whom they have been given to live in proximity.

Service on hiring committees has given way to meetings every Thursday night with an "enemy-love group." Sam launched this group two years ago. The group meets and *practices* enemy love. They share with one another about their deep insecurities and hot buttons. Then they say the most terrible things to one another and treat each other in deplorable ways in order to give occasion for the practice of loving response. It's a creative bunch. And for two hours, they devote their creative energies to the oral infliction of pain and discomfort . . . and with considerable success.

It's a radical idea. And Sam wasn't sure how it would go. Would these people just end up hating one another? But it's bearing fruit.

Folks come to the group each week with stories about how they were able to respond differently to *actual* enemies because of what they had practiced in the class. Trained and practiced maneuvers are finding their way into the natural and spontaneous responses of practitioners in the real world. The group is finding that the habitual response of curse, rejection, and contempt in the face of offense can be gradually replaced by the spontaneous inclination to think of the offender as deeply in need of blessing. They're learning this not through a sermon series on enemy-love but through the painful and risky business of relational sparring, where an offensive maneuver is understood by both partners as an opportunity for practice and training in the Way.

Somehow, Sam's previously narrow scope of concern has expanded to include not only his nuclear family and family of origin but also his neighbors, his brothers and sisters in the faith, and even his enemies and those at the margins of society.

Sam's interaction with the Confucian wisdom tradition has increased and expanded his humanity — his human-ness. He is better situated to delve more deeply into the Way of Jesus than he was ten years ago. He's on a trajectory now that is taking him closer to what he was designed to be. And that's something to be wholeheartedly celebrated.

Of course, these changes in Sam's life could have come to him in some other way. Workaholics often awaken to their condition and make changes without any introduction whatsoever to the Confucian wisdom tradition. And people come in countless ways to the realization that a life without the opportunity for genuine submission will trend in the direction of a narrowing scope of concern. Wonderful! But for Sam, it was that rich tradition stretching back to Confucius that was God's chosen instrument for affecting change for the better. And an apt instrument it is for those of us who have spent whole lives steeped in the values handed down to us from the radical individual-ism characteristic of the contemporary West. Were Sam writing this book, he would wholeheartedly recommend an exploration of the Confucian tradition starting with the *Analects*. And so do I. Read the *Analects* with a few others. Read them slowly and talk about them. See if God might have something for *you* that inspires a deeper under-standing of and engagement with the Way of the Savior, Jesus Christ.

www.ingramcontent.com/pod-product-compliance
Lightning Source LLC
Chambersburg PA
CBHW032007080426
42735CB00007B/531